College in Prison

INFORMATION AND RESOURCES FOR INCARCERATED STUDENTS

Bruce C. Micheals

Order this book online at www.trafford.com
or email orders@trafford.com

Most Trafford titles are also available at major online book retailers.

Printed in the United States of America.

ISBN: 978-1-4269-6453-4 (sc)
ISBN: 978-1-4269-6454-1 (e)

Trafford rev. 04/04/2011

 www.trafford.com

North America & international
toll-free: 1 888 232 4444 (USA & Canada)
phone: 250 383 6864 ♦ fax: 812 355 4082

To the ones we have hurt,
And to the One who heals.

Contents

Acknowledgements

Special thanks to my Lord and Savior, **Jesus Christ,** the timeless example of humility, strength, and wisdom that I pattern my rehabilitation and academic career after. Also I am greatly indebted to my parents, **Bruce and Diane Micheals,** for their continuous support and countless encouragements to consider others, grow in faith, and be productive.

I would be remiss if I failed to thank my college sponsors, who have invested so much in me; so, in no specific order, I thank **John G. Micheals, Nancy A. Quinn, Kermett Spurlock, Jr., Amy L. Micheals, Keith and Val Tinknell, Kermett and Nancy Spurlock, George G. Micheals, Cheryl Torrey** and **Mr. Jon Ullom** (may he always be remembered as a kind and generous man of compassion and concern for his fellow citizen—even a stranger in prison).

Besides my sponsors, I would also like to thank certain individuals who have made special contributions to the advancement of my academic and writing career: my librarian—**Ms. Thompson**—for encouraging me to explore creative writing and the many mysteries of college in prison; my principal—**Ms. Hoag**—for enthusiastically facilitating the development of college level opportunities at Lakeland Correctional Facility; my friend, the director of restorative justice at the **Catholic Diocese of Lansing—Mr. Tim Metts**—for faithfully supporting my work in writing and my goals in education; my friends—**Mr. Tom J. Adams and Ms. Jessica Taylor**—for challenging me to become an asset to society through their organization, Chance For Life, Inc. (CFL) and our motto: "be ye transformed by the renewing of your mind" (Rom 12:2); my local lead-facilitator at CFL--**Sebrell Lee Little** for being unwaveringly committed to the cause of rehabilitative change and academic development; and to my friends **Diana Kopicko** and **Judy Swafford** who converted the hard copy of this manuscript to PDF format when I was at a loss how to get it prepared for publication.

And last, but certainly not least, I thank my college group **Jamie Meade, Ahmad Nelson, Donald Bolton, Robert Coleman, Matthew Martone, Curtis Frye, Bryan Pine, Kris Hook, Scott Wynne, Sheldon Cone Jr., William Espy, Andre Calloway, Camron Coke, Paul Henderson, Joseph Richmond, Tolan Duncan, Nathan Kiehle,** and **Joshua M. Dillon** for joining me in the rehabilitative and academic quest. Your tireless efforts to learn and grow together toward a common goal have made the words of the great philosopher and psychologist William James ring ever more true to me: "We can change our circumstances by a mere change of our attitude." Encouragement, support and contributions by the above mentioned people thoroughly motivated and inspired me to remain committed to this project through more adversity than I care to revisit here. Thank you.

Introduction

When I was 16 years old, I was sentenced to spend the rest of my life in prison for crimes I did in fact commit. I'm 37 now, and though I have more time to serve than most, I seldom consider it enough, enough for what I have done, nor enough for what I am trying to do.

When I came to prison, the days dragged by, each one more of a waste than the last. I tried many of the typical prison activities: gambling, drugs and alcohol, stitches and staples, escape, tear gas, maximum security, long term hole time, etc....But eventually I realized that I was making a fool of myself; I was perpetuating my own destruction. So I made a conscious decision to stop the madness. Later, by the grace of God, I discovered a treasure of educational opportunities that helped transform my prison experience into one of enlightenment, construction, and productivity.

This book, *College in Prison*, is a collection of documents and information regarding what I did to get in school and what I have since learned about other opportunities for college in prison. By the time I finished writing this manuscript, many of my friends and associates successfully used the material provided herein to join me in college; and I hope you will too.

Chapter One

Prepare Yourself For College In Prison

You have made the right decision. College will change your life; I know because it is changing mine. I have been taking correspondence courses since 2005 and the effects of daily study and discipline are remarkable. I have a purpose for every hour of the day--a reason for everything I do--and that purpose enriches my life with a sense of meaning. No longer am I merely doing time, wasting away in a bird cage, as life passes by. Now I am gathering every sour hour, squeezing every precious minute, making a sweet drink that is seldom tasted in prison; and if you follow the instructions presented in this book, you too will be refreshed by the recipe for academic success.

But first, look around for a moment. See the endless games of chess, checkers, and cards that are being played? Now listen to the conversations: numbing banter of boredom that never ceases. Go out to the yard and watch the basketball games, the softball games, the handball games. If they were played in moderation, a game or two per week (or even per day) I wouldn't mention them, but they aren't. They are played incessantly--obsessively--to occupy time and to release energy that will otherwise become stress. But as a drug-dealer turned legitimate entrepreneur once told me: "Play-time is over."

There comes a point in one's incarceration where change may occur. The mentality of the person will dictate the degree and success of the change, but the individual must make a concrete decision to turn off the TV, to retire the chess board, to hang up the jersey. I assume, you, dear reader, have come to this point; and I applaud your awareness of the waste that can come of your incarceration and life if you do not make the change. Some might say your incarceration in itself is a waste, that you should be leading a productive life in society, and who can argue with that? You should be, and so should I; but we aren't. Instead, we are in prison, serving time, determining what the rest of our life will look like. So I encourage you to take stock of your life, measure the person that you are, and choose to be honest, educated and productive.

Chapter Two

The Skills You Need

If you are going to pursue a college education from prison, spend time developing your math, English, and writing skills. Don't be like a guy I know, who assumed he could jump into a college math course without any preparation: he wound up paying for two time extensions and ended up with a D in the course. Now his GPA is wrecked, he is discouraged, and it is going to be harder for him to find people to financially support his college effort. Instead, do like I did and check out a few basic math textbooks from the prison library, and take the tests in them. If you do well, check out some algebra books, and take the tests in them. By testing, you will get an idea of where you stand and of which courses you should take.

Incarcerated students often find math difficult, yet the students who study everyday always seem to catch on. Therefore, my theory is that math is too hard for lazy students who don't study enough. I struggled in my first math course, but I studied hard, for many hours per day at times, and I finished with an A. Incidentally, I also expect to be challenged by my next math course, to have to study even more, and to finish with another A. I believe in keeping a positive attitude and doing the work necessary to finish the job without regrets. If you expect anything less than a challenge from college math, you are setting yourself up for failure.

To prepare for college level math, study everything up to intermediate algebra (algebra two), from there you will be prepared to take and pass developmental mathematics in college—the lowest college course offered in math through most programs. If you are able to test out of the intermediate level of algebra, you will be ready to take college algebra which is a required course for virtually all college degrees.

English, like math, has rules, requiring a significant amount of study time, and is one of the three most important subject skills you are going to need in college. Prior to taking my first English course, I spent six months studying the fundamentals of English from library textbooks. I earned an A in that course also, but I would have done poorly without the months of preparation.

Writing skills are different than English skills. English skills generally denote grammar and punctuation skills; whereas, writing skills indicate styling skills. Styling is the various methods of applying grammar and punctuation to produce attractive and effective sentences, paragraphs, and formats (e.g. essays). Students will write hundreds of essays along the road to a degree; thus, the development of good writing skills is imperative.

Your library should have plenty of math, English, and styling books available; but do yourself a favor and buy a "writers handbook," also. I use <u>Diana Hacker's A Writer's Reference</u> (4th Ed.) from Bedford/St. Martin's (ISBN: 0-312-404161-2). In it I can find all the grammar, punctuation, and styling rules I need, and it has a great section on source citing—a must for college papers. The book is compact, 400+ pages, with tabbed edges for quick reference. Highly recommended.

Chapter Three

Policy

All of the rules regarding college opportunities can be found in the policy directive at your law library. Before you contact anyone, concerning your interest in pursuing academics, you should read the policy and ask yourself some important questions.

1. May a third party pay for my education or does tuition have to be sent directly from my inmate account?

2. What is the process for enrolling in a correspondence course?

3. What restrictions are placed on study aids and supplies at my facility (e.g. scientific calculators, three-ring binders, CD's, etc.)?

4. Am I permitted computer access?

5. What is the standard proctoring procedure?

6. Does the completion of a degree increase my prison pay, or lower my security level, or otherwise affect my life style in prison?

7. Will I be required to maintain full-time employment in the prison if I am a full-time student?

8. Can I get an educational transfer-hold if I do not want to be transferred during my correspondence obligation?

9. Who do I contact if I require a waiver or some other exception to the policy?

Chapter Four

Networking with Other Prisoners

To increase your odds of successfully acquiring a college education, encourage other prisoners to join your quest. At first this suggestion may be unattractive, but consider some of the pros and cons of working toward a college education with other incarcerated students.

Pro: By working together you will have study partners

Con: By working together you have additional responsibilities. For instance, if you become proficient in math the group will automatically call on you when someone needs help with math.

Pro: By working together you will break a long standing stereotype about prisoners, which says we are unable to successfully work toward and complete an honest, productive, common goal that requires significant time and investment.

Con: By working together you will find out just how selfish and corrupt each person in the group is.

Pro: By working together your requests for accommodations, such as, a quiet place to study, extra library time, and funding for materials, will have the weight of numbers.

Con: By working together your reputation with the prison administration will be affected by the actions of the group; for example, if a study room is provided for the college group and one of the students gets caught brewing wine in the room, all of the students will be affected.

Also, by working together you will provide evidence of your interest in contributing to the welfare of your community. Later, if you apply for scholarships, you will benefit from being in a group that displays a strong sense of solidarity. You will be able to show that you understand the advantages of teamwork and that you have developed a social interest.

Once you have determined to include other prisoners in your plans to acquire an education, you should begin talking to people who might contribute to your academic interests. Networking is pro-social; it is opening up to other people and allowing them to open up to you. When done properly—honestly—alliances are formed and you become stronger, more capable of accomplishing your goals. In time, if you study by the light of rehabilitation, you will find other like-minded individuals, and together you will not only become enlightened, but you will enlighten others.

Chapter Five

Gaining Staff Support For Education

The principal of the educational department, the librarian, and the special activities director at your facility, can be of tremendous assistance to you and other incarcerated students. When reaching out to them, be honest, respectful, and patient; by doing so, you will earn their respect and their favor.

The Librarian

A few years ago I joined a writers' group that was held in a prison library on Friday evenings. I wasn't really a writer, poet, or reader at the time; I joined because I was no longer in the criminal life, and I needed some new friends—productive friends. The group was sponsored by the University of Michigan and the facility librarian. About a year after I joined, I began studying math and English while I was raising money to get into college. After my first two courses (which cost $1,125), I decided to research other correspondence programs to find more affordable courses.

At the time, the library kept a file cabinet full of college catalogs, but many of them were outdated; so I asked the librarian for permission to update the cabinet with new catalogs. She said I could, and I began writing letters (See example 1) to every accredited distance learning program I could find. Other prisoners often asked what I was doing, and after I told them, some asked if they too could help; conversely, other prisoners simply complained and bemoaned PELL Grants being discontinued for prisoners and all the correspondence opportunities going online. I listened politely and continued addressing envelopes for the librarian to mail out.

Over the next few months we received current catalogs from more than 100 schools— many of which were happy to serve the correspondence needs of prisoners. The men who helped me with the project exhibited a desire to do positive, constructive things, related to education and together we became The College Group.

Helping the library update the college cabinet, familiarized us with many of the best college opportunities available to prisoners. Therefore, spend time at your library, tell your librarian about your collegiate aspirations, and ask for permission to start (or renovate) a college catalog cabinet. If you get permission, start your cabinet by contacting all of the schools listed in chapter 8 (Distance Learning/Correspondence Programs): simply address the envelopes and stuff them with letters that ask for a few copies of the current "distance learning" catalog, and ask the librarian to mail the letters for you since the materials are for the library.

After I studied the catalogs that arrived, I asked my librarian if the group and I could write some campus bookstores to request textbook donations for the library. She said we were welcome to, and we ended up contacting about 50 bookstores (See example 2). Over the next two months we got about 25 large boxes packed full of new and used college textbooks in a variety of subjects: algebra, calculus, biology, psychology, English, history, public speaking, even casino management. Apparently when professors switch to newer editions of textbooks, the campus bookstores get stuck with the remaining stock of earlier editions—which they are often happy to donate to prison libraries. I wrote the bookstores a thank-you letter (See example 3), and then we began unpacking the boxes. It took months to process all of the books, and because there were so many duplicates, the librarian gave hundreds of them away to prisoners throughout the facility; In fact, I ended up with books on intermediate algebra, algebra/trigonometry, introduction to calculus, linear calculus, biology, western history, and several others, including a few books on writing.

The Principal

Of everyone on staff at your facility, the principal has the most potential to help you. As a student you will go through the principal's office for everything from enrollment to graduation, so it is imperative for you to develop and maintain a good rapport with your principal.

Initially you should write the principal a brief letter (See example 4) expressing your interest in collegiate studies. In your letter request information regarding available post-secondary programs and opportunities, and mention that you have read the relevant policies. Some prisons have college programs—most do not—so you should expect a brief reply that encourages you to seek whatever correspondence opportunities you can afford.

From there, send an official introduction to the principal from you and the other students who are seeking college education (See example 5). Explain who you are, what you have done lately, and what you want from the principal. I suggest asking for nothing—or very little—initially; make the introduction pleasant by being honest, concise, and polite in your letter, but refrain from being less than genuine.

Because prison is concentrated with corrupted people, you may not get a warm reception at first. Don't be discouraged. As ex-felons, ex-criminals, we have the burden of proving our rehabilitation—our integrity—and that takes time, effort, and commitment; however, if you apply yourself, principals will naturally grow to appreciate your interest in academics and rehabilitation.

About a week later, follow-up your introduction with a letter (See example 6) and a newspaper clipping or some other piece of information—an excerpt from this book?—that provides an example of the college programming at a different facility. Express your interest in college programming again, but be brief.

A few weeks later, send another letter (See example 7), an update that describes one or two things college students at your facility need. This is your first request from the principle, so be reasonable. If you don't get a response within a few weeks, send a letter (See example 8) requesting a meeting.

When you meet with the principal be prepared to discuss the following:

1. Why you are interested in getting a college education;

2. What you have done to prepare yourself to participate at the collegiate level;

3. What your college group has accomplished thus far;

4. How you believe a college program can be established at your facility;

5. What you would like the principal to do.

Drafting an agenda can also be helpful in developing organization and focus as the program expands and the administration takes a greater interest in what you are attempting to do (See example 9).

The Special Activities Director

To increase interest in academics at your facility, consider proposing a writing, algebra, or other academics based workshop that can be facilitated by prisoners who are proficient in the designated skill. Avoid suggesting inmates "teach" during these workshops; instead, use the word"facilitate" which simply means "to make easier." Thus, the facilitator of a letter writing workshop makes letter writing easier by explaining techniques for letter writing. This, and other, activities can be supervised and sponsored through your special activities director.

Bruce C. Micheals

(Example 1)

Dear (name of college) Staff,

Please send three distance learning course catalogs for our college catalog filing cabinet. Our library makes your catalog available to hundreds of potential correspondence students. I hope to hear from you soon.

Sincerely,

Bruce C. Micheals, Jr.

Send catalogs to:

LCF Library
141 First St.
Coldwater, MI 49036

College in Prison

(Example 2)

Dear Campus Bookstore Staff,

I am an inmate at a correctional facility; I am writing to ask if you will consider donating any over-stock or outdated textbooks to my facility library. Some of the other prisoners and I are interested in academics, and we would be happy to study materials you are no longer using. The librarian supports this request, and we hope you will also.

Sincerely,

Bruce C. Micheals, Jr.

Please address response to:
LCF library
141 First St.
Coldwater, MI 49036

[**Note:** The names in this document and others featured in College In Prison have been changed.]

B. Micheals #208666 (B-5-11)
T. Wougre # 287543 (C-1-22)
B. Ewge # 135346 (C-4-29)
N. Rinile # 245775 (E1-99)
K. Eadesq #346436 (B-5-16)
A. Hejcop # 365536 (B-5-3)
B. Holbit # 246556 (B-5-38)
C. Dewoi # 255368 (B-5-13)
T. Siwop #515723 (C-3-57)
K. Dswoipoa # 3235684 (E1-120)
G. Dioh #234567 (B-2-16)
A. Hoioic #324532 (C-3-31)
M. Grdyoi #265689 (B-3-40)
J. Kekryse #236575 (B-2-77)

Lakeland Correctional Facility
141 First St.
Coldwater, MI 49036
10/17/07

Bay Mills Community College Bookstore
Attn: Roami Sotie
12214 West Lakeshore Dr.
Brimley, MI 49715

Dear Ms. Sotie,

I am writing in response to your recent donation of college textbooks to the Lakeland Correctional Facility library; in fact, I am writing on behalf of more than a dozen inmates who, like myself, reach out daily to academics for personal development and meaningful change. The English books you donated especially appeal to me, and Mr. Rinile, one of my peers who has an affinity for mathematics (that I am trying desperately to acquire), is thrilled over the volumes of intermediate Algebra.

We prisoners have contacted more than 100 colleges and universities seeking distance learning opportunities, drafted a proposal for the Educational Department at this facility to consider, and acquired a fine selection of materials—thanks to benefactors like you. Our goal is to make college level scholastics a major part of our incarceration. Many of us have lived in maximum security prisons and crack houses and county jail drunk tanks. We are not content to occupy our time with basketballs and TV re-runs; we want to apply

Ourselves—while we are sober—toward building the momentum necessary to carry us into responsible living.

Your donation is appreciated by all of us, and it will probably enrich more than a few of our lives. Thank you for caring.

Sincerely,

B. Micheals #208666 (B-5-11)

T. Wougre # 287543 (C-1-22)

B. Ewge # 135346 (C-4-29)

N. Rinile # 245775 (E1-99)

K. Eadesq #346436 (B-5-16)

A. Hejcop # 365536 (B-5-3)

B. Holbit # 246556 (B-5-38)

C. Dewoi # 255368 (B-5-13)

T. Siwop #515723 (C-3-57)

K. Dswoipoa # 3235684 (E1-120)

G. Dioh #234567 (B-2-16)

A. Hoioic #324532 (C-3-31)

M. Grdyoi #265689 (B-3-40)

J. Kekryse #236575 (B-2-77)

Bruce C. Micheals

(Example 4)

Dear Principal Wings,

I am writing to inquire whether there are any college programs or opportunities available at this facility, I have my GED, and I would like to build on it by acquiring an Associate's degree over the next few years. I checked the policy regarding college programs and correspondence courses, but it doesn't specifically mention individual programs. Therefore, I would appreciate any suggestions or information you might provide regarding how I should proceed.

Thank you for your time and assistance.

Sincerely,

Bruce C. Micheals, Jr.

B. Micheals #208666 (B-5-11)
T. Wougre # 287543 (C-1-22)
B. Ewge # 135346 (C-4-29)
N. Rinile # 245775 (E1-99)
K. Eadesq #346436 (B-5-16)
A. Hejcop # 365536 (B-5-3)
B. Holbit # 246556 (B-5-38)
C. Dewoi # 255368 (B-5-13)
T. Siwop #515723 (C-3-57)
K. Dswoipoa # 3235684 (E1-120)
G. Dioh #234567 (B-2-16)
A. Hoioic #324532 (C-3-31)
M. Grdyoi #265689 (B-3-40)
J. Kekryse #236575 (B-2-77)
10/11/07

LCF Principal Wings

Re: Higher Education Program

Dear Principal Wings,

On September 9, 2007 I (Bruce Micheals) had the pleasure of making your acquaintance. You may recall the occasion, I was called to your office to retrieve my Ohio University English portfolio, and I asked if you would consider a higher education proposal. You assured me that you would. I have since met with my associates to prepare the following.

Background

Over the past few years most of the prisoners listed herein have been trying to gain a better education. Some of us have been fortunate enough to attend classes on campus or enroll in correspondence courses, while others in our group have taken less traditional routes, such as extensively studying textbooks from the library and pursuing available programming.

This past year, however, with the help of Ms. Halo (the librarian); we have contacted over 100 colleges and universities in an effort to locate affordable educational opportunities. Of these schools we have identified one with a department specifically established for the needs of prisoners (Ohio University), as well as seven schools that offer credits for $125.00 or less each: Louisiana State Univ. ($84), Sam Houston Univ. ($80), Western Washington Univ. ($95), Univ. of Idaho ($100),Univ. of Nevada ($125), Oklahoma State Univ. ($125), and Univ. of South Carolina ($125).

However, even the best rate ($70 per credit) is too expensive for most of us; therefore, we are researching additional options, such as:

*CLEP exams. Through this program, students can test-out of an array of courses for $120 a piece and gain equivalent college credits.

*DSST/DANTES exams. Previously used exclusively by the military, DSST exams could offer incarcerated students similar exams as CLEP at approximately the same price.

*Excelsior College exams. Excelsior exams are approximately $200 each, but we feel they are worth looking into

Unfortunately, most universities only permit a limited amount of "exam credits" to be applied toward a degree, and the costs, while much more affordable than traditional correspondence courses, are still too expensive for many incarcerated students. Consequently, we have been researching funding options through a number of financial aid manuals and directories.

We are currently waiting for applications from more than 40 foundations that might fund our educational endeavor, and we are in the process of contacting several other foundations as well. However, while funding for college is an issue, we realize it is not the only issue.

Request

As incarcerated students we need an advocate to support our endeavor. Your acknowledgement in this regard would encourage dialogue and further development of what we hope might become a model among institutional higher education programs—much like the Greyhound program has become.

College in Prison

(Example 5)

We have a general agenda: to find a quiet place to study, to develop an extensive multimedia study library, to facilitate college-prep workshops, etc. But our experience and liberties are sorely limited; therefore, our proposal—our request—is that you help us explore our options.

To overcome the foreseeable obstacles, we will try to be considerate of your time and resources, and we will try to be especially considerate of the institution's concern for security, budget, and available staff, in future proposal submissions. By proceeding in this fashion, we hope to transcend the stereotypes of inmate/staff relations and enter into a relationship based on meaningful exchange of ideas and cooperation.

Details

To date we have contacted 49 college bookstores requesting donations of textbooks and materials; additionally, we plan to make regular purchases of educational materials (at your direction) through the Prisoner Benefit Fund (PBF) in an effort to stock the program with necessary materials.

Considering the thousands of dollars spent annually on professional grade electronic equipment for the LCF music programs; the weight machines, pool tables, and assorted equipment purchased for the recreation department; and various other PBF expenditures, we feel regular funding for scholastic materials that enrich, rather than entertain, is reasonable. Thus, our aim is to acquire, by donation or PBF funding, all materials needed to sustain the program.

Conclusion

Our goal is to become educated. Some of us are entirely honest and living meticulously responsible lives, as a group, while others are entrenched in the battle for rehabilitation. However, as a group, we have invested in an idea and are committed to helping one another. Consequently, now that we have laid the preliminary foundation, we would like you to manage us in building something the facility and inmates alike might benefit from: The Lakeland Correctional Facility's Higher Education Program.

If our request is desirable, I would be happy to present, in print or in person, an itemized account of our immediate goals, issues, and suggested solutions, for your review. As a group, we value your opinion and would like to begin work on this project at your earliest convenience.

Thank you for your time and patience.

Sincerely,

B. Micheals #208666 (B-5-11)   C. Dewoi # 255368 (B-5-13)

T. Wougre # 287543 (C-1-22)   T. Siwpo # 515723 (c-3-57)

B. Ewge # 135346 (C-4-29)   K. Dseoipoa # 3235684 (E1-120)

N. Rinile # 245775 (E1-99)   G. Dioh #234567 (B-2-16)

K. Eadesq #346436 (B-5-16)   A. Hoioic #324532 (C-3-31)

A. Hejcop # 365536 (B-5-3)   M. Grdyoi #265689 (B-3-40)

B. Holbit # 246556 (B-5-38)   J. Kekryse #236575 (B-2-77)

Bruce C. Micheals, Jr.

LCF Principal Wings

Dear Principal Wings,

Enclosed is a copy of a <u>Detroit Free Press</u> article that I hope you will find interesting. As you can see, regaining higher education in prison isn't merely an isolated desire at LCF; however, if we prisoners are to be successful here, your support is critical. Therefore, if there is anything my peers or I can do to foster your favor, at your convenience, please let me know.

Sincerely,

Bruce C. Micheals, Jr.

P.S.

One of the college bookstores (Bay Mills Community College) we wrote last month recently donated a few thousand dollars worth of college textbooks to the LCF library. We expect more donations shortly.

P.S.S.

The Prisoner Benefit Fund intends to vote on a $700 procurement for a college level VCR series on algebra later this month. The inmates unanimously support the request.

B. Micheals #208666 (B-5-11)
T. Wougre # 287543 (C-1-22)
B. Ewge # 135346 (C-4-29)
N. Rinile # 245775 (E1-99)
K. Eadesq #346436 (B-5-16)
A. Hejcop # 365536 (B-5-3)
B. Holbit # 246556 (B-5-38)
C. Dewoi # 255368 (B-5-13)
T. Siwop #515723 (C-3-57)
K. Dswoipoa # 3235684 (E1-120)
G. Dioh #234567 (B-2-16)
A. Hoioic #324532 (C-3-31)
M. Grdyoi #265689 (B-3-40)
J. Kekryse #236575 (B-2-77)

LCF Principal Wings

Re: Higher Education Program

Dear Principal Wings:

I am writing to update you on the progress my peers and I have made in our educational endeavor and to ask for your assistance in two key areas we need help in.

As I have mentioned in previous correspondence, we wrote to 49 college bookstores asking for book donations, and I am happy to report numerous contributions. The library is currently processing dozens of books to be added to an expanded non-fiction section, and based on the responses we received; I do not foresee a lack of study material in the near future.

However, we are still lacking at least two essential elements that would offer us reasonable opportunity for collegiate advancement: (1) a quiet environment conducive to learning, and (2) an affordable option for acquiring college credit.

As you may recall, in September I asked for permission to study in the school building. I must admit, I was being inconsiderate. The fact is, there are at least a dozen students who need a quiet atmosphere in which to study. Therefore, to accommodate us, would you consider designating Ms. Teacher's classroom as a study room when it isn't being used for other purposes? The officer's station is located directly in front of the room, and, considering the proximity to the library, I believe it would make a good study area.

As for affordable college credits, I would like to know whether you will research the possibility of getting LCF authorized to administer CLEP, DSST, or Excelsior exams. As you can see by the enclosed letter, I have been successful in locating an enthusiastic contact person at Excelsior, but CLEP and DSST have been unresponsive to my inquiries.

I originally intended to provide you with material on all three exam options, but under the circumstances, I hope you will find the following acceptable:

1. College Level Examination Program (CLEP) is accepted at nearly 3,000 colleges and universities. The exams cost $110 each. (www.collegeboard.com)

2. DANTES Subject Standardized Tests (DSST) is accepted at less than 2,000 colleges and universities. The exams cost $70 each. (www.getcollegecredit.com)

3. Excelsior College Examination (ECE) is accepted at less than 1,000 colleges and universities. The exams cost about $200 each. (www.excelisors.edu)

Due to their rather expensive and limited selection, Excelsior doesn't actually meet the needs of LCF students, but CLEP and DSST certainly do. Thus, we need you to bring these testing options to LCF. By doing so you will provide means for us to acquire college credits.

Principal Wings, we are trying—desperately trying—to start over in life. We don't want to continue living irresponsibly, and we are looking to academics for a structured, discipline oriented medium in which to reform. Might I add, we aren't being forced—like GED students—to come to you: we are here because we believe academics will help us.

Please consider our needs, and feel free to contact me if I can help with anything further.

Sincerely,

Bruce Micheals #208666 (B-5-11)
P.S. I just got my first college transcript in the mail from Ohio University. For $1,125 I was able to take two courses and earn eight credits; through CLEP I could have earned 30 credits for the same investment.

College in Prison

(Example 8)

Dear Principal Wings, 12/4/07

    I have a number of questions regarding educational opportunities that might be available to LCF students; I have reviewed the policy directive for pertinent information, but answers--if any--were sparse. Some of the questions I have to relate to the following.

- CLEP, DSST, and Excelisior College exams

- Study accommodations

- PBF funding through the educational department for study materials

- Financial aid options that I have found

    Besides questions, I also have news, information, and ideas about institutional collegiate education that I would like to discuss with you. If your schedule permits, please call me out at your convenience.

Sincerely,

Bruce Micheals #208666 (B-5-11)

Bruce C. Micheals

(Example 9)

LCF HIGHER EDUCATION PROGRAM AGENDA

The following goals, issues, potential solutions, and resolutions are offered as a tool for evaluation of where we, incarcerated students, have come from, are now, and wish to go. Revisions, up-dates, and amendments to this agenda will occur as new information, resources, and opportunities become available.

Goal #1:   To identify responsible inmates who wish to incorporate academics into their rehabilitation.

Issues: 1. Inmates often want more than they are willing to earn.

2. The desire for education, by inmates, may be host to illicit intentions (i.e. to become better criminals rather than to become better people).

Solutions: 1. Have one inmate incorporate academics into his rehabilitation.

2. Allow that student to share his experience with other inmates.

3. Observe the contributions (or willingness to contribute) of inmates who want to participate in a higher education program.

4. Ask the inmates whether they intend to pursue an honest, responsible lifestyle.

Resolve: Over the past year more than a dozen LCF inmates have been identified for this program. One inmate set the standard by making an absolute commitment to rehabilitate, enrolling in college (via correspondence), and earning top grades. Others prepared for the challenge of incarcerated college life as well by studying college textbooks from the library, learning foreign languages, participating in rehabilitation based programs such as Criminon and Commitment to Change, ect... Furthermore, all participants have contributed, in some manner, to the development of this program-often through many hours of tedious research and clerical labor.

Goal #2:   To determine the most economical means of acquiring a quality education for the group.

Issues: Many distance learning programs are poorly accredited, require the student to spend time on campus (residency requirement), and charge more than $125.00 per credit.

Solutions: 1. Contact regionally accredited colleges and universities and request their distance learning catalogs.

2. Identify the programs that offer credits at $125 or less.

3. Identify the programs that have no residency requirements for graduation.

4. Investigate alternative measures for incarcerated students to acquire college credits.

Resolve: We have contacted over 100 colleges and universities, identified eight programs with credits for $125 or less, and found several that have no residency requirement for graduation. We are also currently looking into CLEP, DSST/DANTES, and Excelisior College for "test-out "options which are expected to cost a fraction of the traditional amount one might expect to pay for equivalent credits from a correspondence course.

Goal #3   To gain the support of LCF Principal Wings.

Issues: The principal may concentrate on our past misdeeds and present circumstances rather than on the honor of our proposal.

Solution: Provide the principal with at least a year of research, commitment, and results before requesting her support.

Resolve: We began our endeavor in the spring of 2006. For more than a year we have worked together to acquire and analyze information relevant to our goals. On 10/11/07 the principal was presented a concise account of what we have done, are doing, and hope to do in relation to the program.

Goal #4   To encourage a cooperative effort regarding the proposed Higher Education Program, between the school principal, the librarian, and the special activities coordinator.

Issues: Personality conflicts and institutional politics.

Solution: Highlight the value of cooperative effort: fewer burdens on any individual staff member or department, increased institutional respectability, greater potential for development and diversity of the program.

Resolve: The principal's response to the initial proposal is pending; the librarian is supportive; the special activities director is tentatively supportive. The Special Activities Director has only spoken with this writer about the matter once, but he did indicate support if we can navigate the issues such as funding and staff supervision.

Goal #5 To address the logistics of establishing a higher education library of study aids.

Issues: Security, Storage Space, Budget.

Solutions: 1. Security. Limit our requests to media already approved for use at LCF.

2. Storage Space. Store the study aids in the library. The accessibility of the library will give all students, regardless of schedule, sufficient opportunity to use the material

3. Budget. Seek donations and PBF funding.

Resolve: 1. Security. The library already offers books, cassette tapes, and VCR tapes as part of its services. Centralizing our materials there would be an efficient way to utilize existing resources.

2. Storage Space. The librarian told this writer on several occasions that she welcomes donations and PBF funding for educational purchases.

3. Budget. We have sent donation requests to 49 campus bookstores; additionally, the Chairman of the Warden's Forum, PBF members, and various representatives have pledged their support in funding a higher education program.

Goal #6: To acquire a reasonable measure of stability for the students.

Issues: Random transfers might disrupt student's ability to participate in college courses.

College in Prison

(Example 9)

Solution: Seek educational holds for participating students.

Resolve: Per the warden: Students enrolled in college programs may contact her Office to
           receive an educational hold which will keep the inmate-student at this facility for
           the duration of his course(s).

Chapter Six

Prison Politics and the Administration

The Warden, Deputy Warden, and the Assistant Deputy Warden often see the worst prisoners, the prisoners who have given up on life, and the prisoners who—some might say—cannot be helped. You, however, must offer the administration a different example: a positive example. You can do this by communicating with them.

Some prisoners fear communicating with the administration. They fear being falsely accused of being a snitch, they fear being unable to communicate intelligently, they fear rejection. I understand these fears because I had to deal with each of them at one time or another over the past 20 years, and I encourage you to do the same as soon as you are able. If you boldly seek change, the courageous communications of your heart and mind will distinguish you as a leader and a person of integrity who doesn't allow peer pressure to arrest your will to excel.

In time, you will find that the administrative officials are often wrongly cast in a bad light by scorned prisoners. We should understand that just as we pray for the administration to see us as human beings who are capable of both good and evil, so too, must we regard them as such; therefore, when you have made a firm commitment to change, reach-out to the administration and tell them about your decision, so they might see the good heart and mind that is developing in you and others in your facility.

Chapter Seven

Information and Resources

College in prison is attainable through dozens of schools and programs that are as diverse as the subjects they teach. In order to choose the ones that best serve your needs, become familiar with these options. Study this section and you will find numerous examples of college in prison, and while you are studying, be sure to check with your principal and librarian regarding collegiate programs and materials currently available at your facility.

The following chapters will describe the best post-secondary programs, methods, and resources I have found to be available to incarcerated students.

Chapter Eight

Distance Learning/Correspondence Programs I

The following sequence is offered to familiarize you with the distance learning experience.

1. After you have chosen the program you wish to participate in, you will need to send your school principal an enrollment form, a disbursement (a check) for $20-$50 to cover enrollment fees, and a stamped envelope addressed to the school. Enrollment forms are available in most college catalogs. Some programs offer free enrollment.

2. The school may ask you to take an entrance exam; if so, a qualified staff member (principal, teacher, librarian, etc.) can proctor---administer---the tests for you.

3. Once you have been enrolled, you will receive a Personal Identification Number (PIN) and an academic advisor. Print the PIN on all of your correspondence with the school, and consult your academic advisor whenever you have questions regarding your education.

4. Before registering for a course, determine whether it is available in correspondence (print) format; also, find out whether there are any special components or requirements necessary to complete the course, such as, CD-ROM, VCR/DVD, or audio recordings. When registering, send a course registration form, a disbursement for tuition, and a stamped envelope addressed to the school, to your principal for processing. Note that enrolling in a school is different from registering for a course. Registration forms are available in school catalogs.

5. A few weeks after you register for a course you will receive a package of materials that includes a syllabus (instructions for how to take the course) and assorted documents related to your course and the school. Among other things, the syllabus will tell you which books to buy; while waiting for them to arrive, I suggest checking with your library for additional books on the subject.

6. Most correspondence courses have 10-20 lessons and 1-3 exams. The lessons are like homework; you study the material, and you do the assignments. The lessons are submitted

through the mail for a grade that will be a fraction--usually 25%-- of your final grade in the course, and exams will occur periodically as you work through the course. Refer to your syllabus for specific details. Also, all exams must be proctored; that is, all exams must be administered by a responsible person, usually a person in education, who has a higher degree than the one sought by the person taking the exam. It is your responsibility to find and notify the school of who your proctor will be. Generally, principals, teachers, and librarians proctor exams for incarcerated students.

7. After you have completed all of your lessons and exams, you will receive a final grade. Once you have at least one final grade, you can purchase a transcript from the school registrar. A transcript is an official document that attests to your grades. Once you complete your first course(s), get copies of your transcript, and share them with your sponsors (see chapter 13) so they can see how well you have been doing.

8. Once you complete a course, register for another, and continue to take courses until you have accumulated enough credits to earn a degree. Then, apply for graduation, and your degree will be awarded through your principal's office on behalf of your college or university.

If you graduate with a high grade point average (GPA)---usually 3.6 or better on a 4.0 scale---you may qualify for honors distinction: cum laude (with honors), magna cum laude (with great honors), or summa cum laude (with highest praise). Honors are noted on degree diplomas.

Another way to distinguish your academic achievements is to join Delta Epsilon Tau (DET) honor society. For details, contact:

> Distance Education & Training Council
> Delta Epsilon Tau
> 1601 18th Street, N.W.
> Washington, DC 20009

In addition to the above information you should also be aware of the accreditation policy at the school through which you seek a degree. In Prisoners' Guerrilla Handbook to Correspondence Programs in the United States and Canada Jon Marc Taylor elaborates on accreditation, saying:

Accreditation by a U.S. Department of Education recognized accrediting agency assures a student that the "accredited school" has met certain standards concerning the quality of education, faculty qualifications, appropriate text and materials, financial stability, etc. Earning course credits at one accredited school generally assures the transferability of those classes to another college, excepting that particular institution's policies and curriculum.

There is no one national accrediting agency. There are six regional associations and the Distance Education & Training Council (DETC), which generally accredits independent and proprietary schools. If those schools you are interested in are accredited by any of these listed associations, you can be assured of transferable credits and a recognized degree.

These are the accreditation agencies recognized by the U.S. Department of Education:

Middle States Association of Schools & Colleges
New England Association of Schools & Colleges
North Central Association of Colleges & Schools
Northwest Association of Schools & Colleges
Southern Association of Schools & Colleges
Western Association of Schools & Colleges
Distance Education & Training Council

Besides accreditation, you should also find out what the residency requirements are at your school. Residency requirements are the school policies regarding how much time a student must spend on campus to graduate. Most schools allow students to do courses entirely by correspondence without any campus time; some schools even allow students to earn degrees entirely by correspondence without any campus time. The accreditation and residency requirements of several colleges and universities throughout the United States will be listed in the next chapter along with information regarding tuition, course selection, degree options, etc.

Chapter Nine

Distance Learning/Correspondence Programs II

Shopping in prison for a good college program is challenging. Among other things, you will need to determine whether the program you are interested in is regionally accredited, what degrees are offered (if any), how much tuition and related fees are, what courses are offered, and what the residency requirements are.

This chapter will introduce you to the best distance learning college programs available to incarcerated students today. All of the programs featured herein are regionally accredited and none of the degree programs have residency requirements (that is, degrees can be earned entirely by correspondence).

TOP 5 MOST AFFORDABLE DISTANCE LEARNING DEGREE PROGRAMS

Rank/School	Approx. Cost Per Course
1. Adams State College	$360
2. Vincennes University	$434
3. Indiana University	$461
4. University of Northern Iowa	$552
5. Ohio University	$562
Honorable Mention: California State University (2)	------
Honorable Mention University of North Dakota	------
Honorable Mention: University of Manitoba (Canada) (3)	------

TOP 25 MOST AFFORDABLE DISTANCE LEARNING COURSE PROGRAMS

Rank/School	Approx.Cost Per Course
1. Sam Houston State University	$240
2. Louisiana State University	$262
3. Western Washington University(4)	$305
4. University of Idaho	$325
5. Oklahoma State University	$355
6. Adams State University	$360
7. Vincennes University	$434
8. Indiana University	$461
9. Chadron State University	$471
10. University of Nevada-Reno	$474
11. Texas State University	$510
12. University of Florida	$549
13. University of Northern Iowa	$552
14. Southern Illinois University-Carbondale	$555

15.	Ohio University (1)	$562
16.	University of Central Arkansas	$598
17.	Northern State University	$610
18.	University of Mississippi	$639
19.	University of Nebraska	$651
20.	University of Colorado-Boulder	$675
21.	University of North Dakota	$695
22.	University of Missouri	$708
23.	University of North Carolina (5,6)	$750
24.	University of Kansas	$754
25.	University of Illinois	$840

1. Price includes book, postage, and supplies; test-out option: $276 per course

2. CSU is one of the only schools to offer a Master's degree via correspondence

3. Check U of M's international tuition rates before enrolling.

4. WWU will design courses to meet your needs; ask about "contract study."

5. Tuition discounts are available to in-state students.

6. Test-out option: $250 per course ($117 for in-state students)

Bruce C. Micheals

ADAMS STATE COLLEGE
OFFICE OF EXTENDED STUDIES
208 EDGEMONT BLVD
ALAMOSA, CO 81102
1-800-548-7974
www.exstudies.adams.edu

Accreditation:	North Central Association of Colleges & Schools

External Degrees:
1. Associates of Arts
2. Associates of Science
3. Bachelor of Arts-Business Administration
4. Bachelor of Science-Business Administration/General Business
5. Bachelor of Science-Business Administration/Management
6. Bachelor of Science-Business Administration/MIS
7. Bachelor of Science-Business Administration/Legal Studies
8. Bachelor of Arts-Sociology/Criminology
9. Bachelor of Arts-Sociology/Criminology Corrections
10. Bachelor of Arts-Sociology/Criminology Law Enforcement
11. Bachelor of Arts-Sociology/Social Welfare
12. Bachelor of Arts-Sociology/Social Work

Tuition and Fees: $120 per credit hour/ $360 per course

Time Limit: One year and optional $35 three months extension

Courses: Art 1, Business 27, Criminal Justice 9, Economics 2, Education 1, English 19, Environmental Science 1, Exercise Physiology, Leisure Science 1, Geology 1, Government 4, History/Government/Philosophy 2, History 8, Interdivisional 2, Math 7, Philosophy 1, Psychology 1, Sociology 28.

Comments: ASC accepts up to 45 transfer credits to be applied to an associate's degree and up to 90 transfer credits to be applied to a bachelor's degree. ASC also accepts CLEP.

CALIFORNIA STATE UNIVERSITY-DOMINGUEZ HILLS
HUMANITIES MASTER OF ARTS (HUX)
1000 EAST VICTORIA STREET-SAC 2-2126
CARSON, CA 90747
(310) 243-3743
www.csudh.edu/hux

Accreditation: Western Association of Schools & Colleges

External Degrees: 1. Master of Arts-Humanities/History
                        2. Master of Arts-Humanities/Literature
                        3. Master of Arts-Humanities/Music
                        4. Master of Arts-Humanities/Art
                        5. Master of Arts-Humanities/Philosophy

Tuition and Fees: $6,360 (30 units at $212 per unit)

Time Limit: Up to five years

Comments: The CSU Master of Arts program provides an exceptionally rare
                        opportunity for incarcerated students to earn graduate degrees via
                        correspondence. This program is arguably the crown jewel of college
                        in prison.

Bruce C. Micheals

CHADRON STATE COLLEGE
CORRESPONDENCE PROGRAM
1000 MAIN STREET
CHADRON, NE 69337
1-800-242-3766
www.csc.edu

Accreditation: North Central Association of Colleges & Schools

Tuition and Fees: $157 per credit hour/$471 per course

Time Limit: One year

Courses: Accounting 2, Economics 3, English 4, Geosciences 1, Industrial Technology 2, Mathematics 1

College in Prison

INDIANA UNIVERSITY
INDEPENDENT STUDY
OWEN HALL 001
790 E. KIRKWOOD AVE.
BLOOMINGTON, IN 47405-7101
1-800-334-1011
www.scs.indiana.edu

Accreditation:	North Central Association of Colleges & Schools
External Degrees:	1. Associates of Arts-General Studies 2. Bachelor of General Studies
Tuition and Fees:	$132.00 per credit hour plus $65.00 per course plus course Learning guide fee / $461 per course
Time limit	One year and optional six months extension
Courses:	Anthropology 4, Arts and Sciences (Career Development) 1, Astronomy 3, Biology 2, Business 25, Classical Studies 5, Communication and Cultures 3, Comparative Literature 3, Computer Science 1, Criminal Justice 5, Economics 3, Education 4, English 27, Fine Arts 2, Folklore and Ethnomusicology 3, French 2, Gender Studies 1, Geography 5, Geological Science 4, Health 6, History 22, History and Philosophy Of Science 1, Journalism 2, Linguistics 1, Mathematics 9, Music 3, Near Eastern Languages and Culture 2, Nursing 1, Philosophy 7, Physics 3, Political Science 6, Psychological and Brain Science 6, Religious Studies 5, Sociology 9, Spanish 4.

Bruce C. Micheals

LOUISIANA STATE UNIVERSITY
CONTINUING EDUCATION
1225 PLEASANT HALL
BATON ROUGE, LA 70803-1500
1-800-234-5046
www.is.1su.edu

Accreditation: Southern Association of Colleges and Schools

Tuition and Fees: $84 per credit hour plus $10 processing fee/$262 per Course

Time Limit: Nine months and optional $25 three month extension

Courses: Accounting 10, African & African American Studies 1, Anthropology 2, Biological Sciences 2, Business Law 2, Classical Studies 1, Communication Studies 1, Curriculum And Instruction 1, Dairy Science 1, Economics 5, Education 1. English 17, Environmental Studies 2, Finance 2. French 4, Geology 2, German 5, History 9, Human Resources Education 4, Information Systems 1, Kinesiology 3, Latin 2, Management 4, Marketing 8, Mass Communications 1, Mathematics 15, Military Science 1, Music 1, Philosophy 2, Physical Science 2 Physics 2, Political Science 5, Psychology 8, Religious Studies 1, Sociology 5, Spanish 5, Theatre 1, Women's & Gender Studies 1

Comments: Degree seeking students can save thousands on tuition by taking courses through LSU and later transferring the credits to a degree program. Combine LSU courses with CLEP for even greater savings.

College in Prison

NORTHERN STATE UNIVERSITY
OFFICE OF EXTENDED STUDIES
SPAFFORD HALL 106
1200 SOUTH JAY STREET
ABERDEEN, SD 57401
(605) 626-2568
www.northern.edu/extension/index.htm

Accreditation:	North Central Association of Colleges & Schools
Tuition and Fees:	$203.50 per credit hour/ $610.50 per course
Time Limit:	Either 175 days or 350 days and optional $20 three Month's extension
Courses:	Business 8, Education 4, Industrial Technologies 3, Mathematics 7, Sociology 2, Spanish 8

Bruce C. Micheals

OHIO UNIVERSITY
INDEPENDENT AND DISTANCE LEARNING—CPI
HANING HALL 222
ATHENS, OH 45701-2979
1-800-444-2910
www.ohio.edu/independent/

Accreditation:	North Central Association of Colleges & Schools

External Degrees:

1. Associate in Arts-Social Science
2. Associate in Arts-Arts and Humanities
3. Associate in Arts-Science
4. Associate in Individualized Studies
5. Associate in Applied Business
6. Bachelor of Specialized Studies

Tuition and Fees: Comprehensive tuition fee $1,125 per eight credits

Time Limit: Eight months and optional free four months extension

Courses: Accounting 4, African American Studies 2, Aviation 5, Biological Science 4, Business Law 5, Business Management Technology 13, Classics and World Religions 3, Communication Studies 1, Economics 8, English 21, Humanities 6, Finance 1, History 11, Human and Consumer Science 3, International Literature 2, Journalism 2, Law Enforcement Technology 4, Management 1, Marketing 2, Mathematics 13, Medical Assisting Technology 1, Music 2, Office Technology 1, Philosophy 6, Physical Education 2, Physical Science 3 Physics 6, Political Science 1, Professional Communication 1, Psychology 11, Quantitative Business Analysis 1, Sociology 6, Specialized Studies 1, Theater 3, Travel and Tourism 1

Comments: College Program for the Incarcerated (CPI) at Ohio University was established in 1973 to offer prisoners an opportunity to enrich their rehabilitation through education. By providing everything necessary-- from textbooks to rulers--in a single package, CPI effectively empowered incarcerated students who were previously challenged to acquire individual components to college courses. However, CPI uses what is known as quarter credit system which assigns four (or sometimes five) credits per course. This confuses some students, who are only familiar with the semester credit system which assigns three (or sometimes 4) credits per course. Neither the large nor the small CPI catalog addresses this; but, as you can see by the formula below, converting credits from one system to another is fairly easy.

If you have semester credits to transfer to a quarter credit program, multiply the credits by 1.5 to get the quarter credit translation (e.g. 10 semester credits multiplied by 1.5 equals 15 quarter credits). If you have quarter credits to transfer to a semester credit program, divide the credits by 1.5 to get the semester credit translation (e.g. 15 quarter credits divided by 1.5 equals 10 semester credits).

To save money on tuition, take advantage of CPI's Course Credit by Examination (CCE) option. For additional savings, take lesser priced courses through other programs and transfer the credits to CPI. For the greatest savings, transfer CLEP results to CPI for credit before you register for your first CPI course.

Bruce C. Micheals

OKLAHOMA STATE UNIVERSITY
INDEPENDENT STUDY OFFICE
309 WES WATKINS CENTER
STILLWATER, OK 74078
(405) 744-6390
www.osuoutreach.okstate.edu/ics

Accreditation: North Central Association of Colleges & Schools

Tuition and Fees: $118 per credit hour plus $10 shipping fee/ $364 per course

Time Limit: One year and optional $35 six months extension

Courses: Accounting 2, Animal Science 6, Anthropology 1, Business
                          Administration 3, Business Communication 2, Communication
                          Disorders 1, Career Psychology 1, Economic 7, Education 1, Electronics
                          3, English 13, Educational Psychology 3, Finance 1, French 2,
                          Geography 8, German 2, Human Development 3, Health 2, History
                          19, Horticulture 1, Journalism 1, Business Law 2, Mathematics 9,
                          Management 4, Marketing 2, Nutrition1, Political Science 3, Psychology
                          2, Sociology 2, Spanish 3, Statistics 7

College in Prison

SAM HOUSTON STATE UNIVERSITY
CORRESPONDENCE COURSE DIVISION
BOX 2536
HUNTSVILLE, TX 77341-2536
(936) 294-1005
www.cor.shsu.edu

Accreditation: Southern Association of Colleges & Schools

Tuition and Fees: $70 per credit hour plus $30 for each course/$240 per Course

Time Limit: One year and optional $25 six months extension

Courses: Accounting 2, Agriculture 2, Art 1, Economics 3, English 12, Family & Consumer Science 4, Finance 3, General Business Administration 4, Geography 4, Health 3, History 6, Kinesiology 3, Management 2, Marketing 2, Mathematics 4, Philosophy 1, Photography 1, Political Science 2, Psychology 2, Sociology 6, Statistics 2

Comments: SHSU offers the most affordable regionally accredited correspondence courses in the United States. Incarcerated students can save thousands of dollars on tuition by taking SHSU courses and later transferring the credits to a degree program.

Bruce C. Micheals

SOUTHERN ILLINOIS UNIVERSITY-CARBONDALE
DIVISION OF CONTINUING EDUCATION
MAIL CODE 6705
703 S. WASHINGTON STREET
CARBONDALE, IL 62901
(618) 536-7751
www.dce.siu.edu/siuconnected

Accreditation:	North Central Association of Colleges & Schools
Tuition and Fees:	$185 per credit hour/ $555 per course
Time Limit:	Twenty weeks (extension available)
Courses:	Administration of Justice 5, Allied Health 1, Anthropology 1, Arts 3, Educational Psychology 1, English 2, Finance 4, Foreign Languages and Literature 4, General Agriculture 2, Geography 1, Health Education 2, History 2, Kinesiology 1, Mathematics 2, Management 3, Philosophy 1, Political Science 8, Women's Studies 2

College in Prison

TEXAS STATE UNIVERSITY-SAN MARCOS
OFFICE OF CORRESPONDENCE AND EXTENSION STUDIES
601 UNIVERSITY DRIVE
SAN MARCOS, TX 78666-4616
(512) 245-2322
www.studyanywhere.txstate.edu

Accreditation:	Southern Association of Colleges & Schools
Tuition and Fees:	$190 per credit hour/$510 per course
Time Limit:	Nine months and optional $35 three months extension
Courses:	Art & Design 1, Biology 1, Business Law 1, Criminal Justice 1, Dance 1, English 13, Health Information Management 1, History 9, Mass Communication 1, Mathematics 6, Music 1, Philosophy 2, Political Science 5, Psychology 7, Sociology 3, Spanish 5, Theatre Arts 1

Bruce C. Micheals

UNIVERSITY OF CENTRAL ARKANSAS
DIVISION OF ACADEMIC OUTREACH EXTENDED STUDY PROGRAM
BREWER-HEGEMAN CONFERENCE CENTER, SUITE 102
201 DONAGHEY AVE.
CONWAY, AR 72035
(501) 450-3118

Accreditation: North Central Association of Colleges & Schools

Tuition and Fees: $199.50 per credit hour/ $598.50 per Course

Time Limit: Six months and optional $120 six months extension

Courses: Accounting 2, Family and Consumer Science 1, Political Science 4,
                      History 5, Mathematics 2, Psychology 4, Sociology 2

College in Prison

UNIVERSITY OF COLORADO-BOULDER
DIVISION OF CONTINUING EDUCATION AND PROFESSIONAL STUDIES
1505 UNIVERSITY AVE.
178 UCB
BOULDER, CO 80309-0178
1-800-331-2801
www.colorado.edu/cewww

Accreditation: North Central Association of Colleges & Schools

Tuition and Fees: $225 per credit hour/ $675 per course

Time Limit: One year and optional $60---per credit hour ---one year extension

Courses: Anthropology 5, English 4, History 2, Mathematics 6, Music 1, Philosophy 3, Political Science 2, Psychology 1

Bruce C. Micheals

UNIVERSITY OF FLORIDA
DIVISION OF CONTINUING EDUCATION
CORRESPONDENCE STUDY
2209 NW 13TH ST., SUITE D
GAINESVILLE, FL 32609
1-800-327-4218
www.correspondencestudy.ufl.edu

Accreditation: Southern Association of Colleges & Schools

Tuition and Fees: $153 per credit hour plus $90 per course/$549 per course

Time Limit: One year

Courses: Advertising 1, Anthropology 1, Business 3, Criminology And Law 6, Economics 2, Education 6, English 14, English (as a second language) 1, Geography 2, Geology 3, History 2, Journalism 1, Latin Language and Literature 1, Linguistics 1, Mathematics 4, Philosophy 2, Political Science 2, Psychology 6, Public Relations 1, Religion 2, Romance Languages 3, Sociology 2, Statistics 2, Study Skills 1

Comments: In state tuition is $108.55 per credit hour plus $90 per Course/ $415 per course

UNIVERSITY OF IDAHO
INDEPENDENT STUDIES
NORTH CAMPUS CENTER (NCC), SUITE 203
645 W. PULLMAN ROAD
P.O. BOX 443225
MOSCOW, ID 83844-3225
(877) 464-3246
www.uidaho.edu/isi

Accreditation: Northwest Association of Schools & Colleges

Tuition and Fees: $100 per credit hour plus $25 per course/ $325 per course

Time Limit: One year and optional $75 six months extension

Courses: Accounting 1, Anthropology 2, Business Law 1, Economics 3, Education 4, English 7, Family and Consumer Sciences 1, Finance 1, Foreign Languages and Literatures 1, Health Care Administration 1, History 9, Journalism and Mass Media 1, Library Science 2, Mathematics 6, Microbiology 1, Museology 2, Physics 4, Political Science 3, Psychology 8, Real Estate 2, Social Science 1, Sociology 4

Bruce C. Micheals

UNIVERSITY OF ILLINOIS-URBANA-CHAMPAIGN
OFFICE OF CONTINUING EDUCATION/GUIDED INDIVIDUAL STUDY
302 EAST JOHN STREET, SUITE 1406
CHAMPAIGN, IL 61820
1-800-252-1360 (ext. 31321)

Accreditation: North Central Association of Colleges & Schools

Tuition and Fees: $256 per credit hour plus $41 per course administrative fee plus $30
                         per course instructional fee/$840 per course

Time Limit: Nine months and optional $100 three months extension

Courses: Classical Civilization 1, English 2, French 4, German 2, History 2,
                         Mathematics 5

College in Prison

UNIVERSITY OF KANSAS
INDEPENDENT STUDY
CONTINUING EDUCATION
1515 ST. ANDREWS ST.
LAWRENCE, KS 66047-1625
(877) 404-5823
www.continuinged.ku.edu/is

Accreditation:	North Central Association of Colleges & Schools
Tuition and Fees:	$251 per credit hour/ $754 per course
Time Limit:	Nine months and optional three months extension
Courses:	Applied Behavioral Science 3, English 7, History 1, Latin 3, Mathematics 6, Philosophy 1, Psychology 2, Spanish 1, Speech and Language Disorders 1, Education 1

Bruce C. Micheals

UNIVERSITY OF MANITOBA
DISTANCE AND ONLINE EDUCATION
188D EXTENDED EDUCATION COMPLEX
WINNIPEG, MANITOBA
R3T 2N2 CANADA
1-888-216-7011 (ext. 8012)
www.umanitoba/ca/distance

Accreditation: N/A

External Degrees: 1. Bachelor of Arts 2. Bachelor of Arts-Geography 3. Bachelor of Social
                      Work 4. Post-Baccalaureate Diploma in Education

Tuition and Fees: $115-$133 per credit hour/$345-$399 per course

Time Limit;   Approx. 13 weeks

Courses: $115 pch; Anthropology 5, Classics 2, Economics 5, English 4, History
                      7, Native Studies 2, Philosophy 3, Political Studies 5, Psychology 15,
                      Religion 3, Sociology 8; $133 pch; Environment and Geography 8,
                      Geological Sciences 3; $124 pch; Educational Administration 7; $128
                      pch: Family Social Science 1, Comments: Students have nine years
                      to earn the Post-Baccalaureate Diploma in Education. Additionally,
                      undergraduate international students are subject to an international
                      differential fee of 180%; however, the Post-Baccalaureate Diploma
                      in Education is a graduate degree and therefore exempt from the
                      international differential fee.

College in Prison

UNIVERSITY OF MISSISSIPPI
INDEPENDENT STUDY
P.O. BOX 729
UNIVERSITY, MS 38677-0729
(877) 915-7313
www.indstudy.olemiss.edu

Accreditation:Southern: Association of Colleges & Schools

Tuition and Fees: $213 per credit hour/$639 per course

Time Limit: One year (extension available)

Courses: Accounting 3, Art 2, Biology 2, Business 1, Chemistry 3, Criminal Justice 3, Economics 1, Education 12, English 10, Family and Consumer Sciences 2, Finance 3, French 4, German 4, History 2, Health Promotion 3, Journalism 1, Legal Studies2, Library Science 1, Marketing 3, Mathematics 2, Park & Recreation Management 3, Philosophy 6, Portuguese 4, Religion 3, Spanish 4, Telecommunications 1, Wellness 1

Bruce C. Micheals

UNIVERSITY OF MISSOURI
CENTER FOR DISTANCE AND INDEPENDENT STUDY
136 CLARK HALL
COLUMBIA, MO 65211-4200
1-800-609-3727
www.cdis.missouri.edu

Accreditation:	North Central Association of Colleges & Schools
Tuition and Fees:	$229 per credit hour plus $20 per course/$708 per course
Time Limit:	Nine months and optional $35 three months extension
Courses:	Accounting 2, Animal Science 2, Anthropology 2, Astronomy 1, Atmospheric Science 1, Biological Engineering 1, Black Studies 1, Economics 4, Education 8, Engineering 2 English 16, French 2, Geography 2, Geological Science 1, History 3, Human Development and Family Studies 2, Latin 2, Management 2, Mathematics 6, Philosophy 3, Physical Education 1, Psychology 2, Spanish 1, Women's and Gender Studies 1

College in Prison

UNIVERSITY OF NEBRASKA-LINCOLN
EXTENDED EDUCATION AND OUTREACH
900 N. 22ND STREET
LINCOLN, NE 68588-8802
(402) 472-2175
www.independentstudy.unl.edu

Accreditation: North Central Association of Colleges & Schools

Tuition and Fees: $192.25 per credit hour plus $75 per course/$651.75 per course

Time Limit: One year and optional $65 three months extension

Courses: Accounting 1, Agricultural Economics 2, Art and Art History 1, Biological Sciences 1, Business Law 1, Chemistry 1, Child and Family Studies 1, Classics 1, Economics 4, English 5, Finance 3, Geography 3, History 6, Industrial and Management Systems Engineering 1, Management 8, Marketing 1, Mathematics 3, Nutrition and Health Sciences 1, Physics 4, Political Science 5, Psychology 6

Bruce C. Micheals

UNIVERSITY OF NEVADA-RENO
INDEPENDENT LEARNING/050
EXTENDED STUDIES
RENO, NV 89557
1-800-233-8928
www.istudy.unr.edu

Accreditation:	Northwest Association of Schools & Colleges
Tuition and Fees:	$138 per credit hour plus $60 per course/ $474 per course
Time Limit:	One year (extension available)
Courses:	Anthropology 2, Counseling and Educational Psychology 1, English 6, Basque 4, French 4, German 4, Italian 4, Spanish 3, Health Ecology 1, History 5, Mathematics 9, Music 1, Nutrition 1, Political Science 3, Psychology 1

College in Prison

UNIVERSITY OF NORTH CAROLINA
INDEPENDENT STUDIES
CB+ 1020 THE FRIDAY CENTER
CHAPEL HILL, NC 27599-1020
1-800-862-5669
www.fridaycenter.unc.edu

Accreditation: Southern Association of Colleges & Schools

Tuition and Fees: $250 per credit hour / $750 per course

Time Limit: Nine months and optional $30 four months extension

Courses: Accounting 1, African Studies 1, Anthropology 1, Art 2, Biology 2, Business 2, Chemistry 4, Classics 2, Economics 2, English 12, Environmental Science 1, Geography 3, Health Education 1, History 12, Hospital Management 1, Italian 4, Latin 1, Mathematics 8, Nursing 1, Philosophy 1, Political Science 3, Psychology 2, Russian 1, Sociology 7, Spanish 6, Statistics2

Comments: In state tuition is $117 per credit hour/$351 per course. For Additional savings, test out of courses through the Course Credit by Examination (CCE) option.

                    CCE (Out of state): $250
                    CCE (In state): $117

Bruce C. Micheals

UNIVERSITY OF NORTH DAKOTA
DIVISION OF CONTINUING EDUCATION
GUSTAFSON HALL----ROOM 103
3264 CAMPUS ROAD STOP 9021
GRAND FORKS, ND 58202-9021
1-800-342-8230
www.conted.und.edu/correspondence

Accreditation: North Central Association of Colleges & Schools

External Degrees: 1. Bachelor of General Studies
                   2. Bachelor of Arts-Social Science

Tuition and Fees: $218 per credit hour and $40 per course/$695 per course

Time Limit: Nine months and optional $35 three months extension

Courses: Anthropology 2, Art 3, Chemical Engineering 1, Communication 2,
                   English Language & Literature 4, French 1, Geography 1, Geology
                   1, History 6, Mathematics 9, Music 1, Psychology 3, Teaching &
                   Learning 2

Comments: The Bachelor's degrees available through correspondence at UND
                   require 125 credits to complete. Students are only required to earn 30
                   of the credits from UND; the remaining credits can be transferred in
                   from more affordable programs.

UNIVERSITY OF NORTHERN IOWA
GUIDED INDEPENDENT STUDY
2637 HUDSON RD.
CEDAR FALLS, IA 50614-0223
1-800-772-1746
www.uni.edu/continuinged/gis

Accreditation: North Central Association of Colleges & Schools

External degrees: 1. Bachelor of Liberal Studies

Tuition and Fees: $184 per credit hour/$552 per course

Time Limit: Nine months and optional $15 three months extension

Courses: Accounting 2, Communications Studies 2, Family Studies 4, Economics 1, Education 14, Educational Psychology 3, English 2, Geography 4, Humanities 6, Marketing 1, Mathematics 3, Music 2, Psychology 1, Religion 2, Social Science 1, Social Work 3, Sociology and Criminology 13

Bruce C. Micheals

VINCENNES UNIVERSITY
DIVISION OF CONTINUING STUDIES
CLASSROOM BUILDING A
1002 NORTH FIRST STREET
VINCENNES, IN 47591
1-800-880-7961
www.vinu.edu/distance

Accreditation: North Central Association of Colleges & Schools

External Degrees: 1. Associate in Arts
                        2. Associate of Applied Science
                        3. Associate of Science

Tuition and Fees: $144.66 per credit hour/$433.98 per course

Time Limit: One year and optional $50 six months extension

Courses: Accounting 3, Economic 1, English 5, Earth Science 1, History 4,
                        Humanities 1, Law Enforcement 4, Mathematics 1, Management 3,
                        Political Science 2, Psychology 2, Sociology 1, Speech 2

WESTERN WASHINGTON UNIVERSITY
EXTENDED EDUCATION AND SUMMER PROGRAMS
MS 5293
516 HIGH STREET
BELLINGHAM, WA 98225-5996
(360) 650-3650
www.extendeded.wwu.edu/ilearn

Accreditation: North Central Association of Colleges & Schools

Tuition and Fees: $95 per credit hour plus $20 per course/$305 per course

Time Limit: Nine months and optional $35 three months extension

Courses: Anthropology 4, Canadian-American Studies 1, Classical Studies 1, Communication 1, Decision Science 1, East Asian Studies 1, Economics 4, Education 1, Engineering Technology 1, English 21, Environmental Science 2, Environmental Studies 4, Greek 1, History 4, Latin 1, Liberal Studies 2, Library Science 1, Management Information Systems 1, Mathematics 5, Mongolian 3, Music 1, Psychology 3, Sociology 5, Women's Studies 1

Chapter Ten

Earn Credits and Save Money: Test-Out

Exam options are one of the best kept secrets in higher education. By "testing-out" of college courses you can save thousands of dollars on tuition while earning transferable college credits. Using this option is like choosing to skip the course assignments and proceeding to the final exam. Generally, exams cost about one quarter to one half as much as standard correspondence courses, and in most cases you can even eliminate your second largest expense—book costs—by studying out of the library. So how does the exam process work? It's really quite simple: (1) the student orders an exam, (2) the exam is sent to a proctor who then administers it, and (3) the student transfers the exam results to a college or university for credit. For example, suppose you take and pass a history exam rather than taking and passing a history course. In taking and passing the exam rather than the course you will have saved hundreds of dollars on books and tuition while earning just as many credits as you would have earned by taking the course.

At this point, you might be thinking: If it's such a great opportunity, why isn't everyone doing it? Well, according to recent College Level Examination Program (CLEP) literature, over 2,900 colleges and universities award credits for passing CLEP exams, so perhaps everyone is doing it. Nevertheless, you should note that most schools only allow students to apply exam credits to 25%-75% of the total credits needed for a degree (e.g. 15-45 exam credits may be applied to a 60 credit Associate's degree).

Also, passing exams isn't easy. Unlike with correspondence courses, exam students are not provided instructor, assignments, or syllabus. Exams are often referred to as challenge courses because, to prepare for them, students often have to step up to the challenge of independently completing the equivalent of an entire course prior to taking the exam.

The following are some of the best exam options available.

College Level Examination Program (CLEP) exams cost $122 each ($10 extra for exams that require an essay). Currently the following 14 exams are available in paper and pencil format for incarcerated students.

Analyzing and Interpreting Literature
College Algebra
College Mathematics
English Composition
Freshman College Composition
History of the United States I: Early Colonization to 1877
History of the United States II; 1865 to the present
Humanities

Information Systems and Computer Applications
Management, Principles of
Natural Science
Psychology, Introductory
Social Sciences and History
Sociology, Introductory

To learn more about CLEP ask your principal to contact:

Thomson Prometric
Attention: CLEP Testing Program
2000 Lenox Drive 3rd Floor
Lawrenceville, NJ 08648
(609) 895-5011
www.collegeboard.com/clep

To make CLEP exams available at your facility, ask your principal to apply for authorization to administer the exams through the contact person below;

Janet F. Swandol
Associate Director, CLEP
Higher Education Services
The College Board
1545 Raymond Diehl Road, Suite 250
Tallahassee, FL 32308
(850) 521-4919

To order the CLEP Official Study Guide, 19th Edition for $24.95 (plus $5.00 s/h) call 1-800-323-7155 This study guide covers all 34 exams offered by CLEP; however, to get a more detailed treatment of your subject, I suggest ordering individual CLEP study guidesrelevant to the exams you intend to take.

Course Credit by Examination (CCE), which is similar to CLEP exams, is offered by Ohio University (OU) for $69 per credit per exam (e.g. a four credit course would cost $276). Currently, OU offers 96 CCE exams in paper-and-pencil format.

However, students who intend to get a degree through OU should note that OU only accepts CLEP credits from students who have not previously taken any OU courses. To learn more about OU and their CCE option, request a copy of their catalog entitled College Program for the Incarcerated (CPI).

Excelsior College Exams are another economical option. There are currently 31 three credit exams available in paper-and-pencil format for $205 each. Request a copy of Excelsior College Examinations Registration Guide and Distance Education Degree Programs for Adult Learners from the address below:

Excelsior College
7 Columbia Circle
Albany, NY 12203-5159

To make these exams available at your facility, ask your principal to contact the testing programs manager at Excelsior College (888-647-2388, enter 1-6-6 at the automated greeting) for authorization to administer Excelsior College Exams.

Chapter Eleven

Experiential Learning Credits

Many colleges award credits for knowledge acquired through life experience. Adult students will likely find "life experience" credits useful in decreasing the cost of college and expediting the process of earning a degree.

There is no universal standard for determining what you can get credit for or how many credits you will receive; however, credit is typically awarded if the knowledge under evaluation is equivalent to what a college student is expected to learn. For instance, fluency in a foreign language, starting or managing a small business, writing a book, learning CPR, earning certificates in drug and alcohol abuse, membership in a band, leading a church group, and many other experiences may be awarded credit if you have sufficient documentation to support your claim to the knowledge. Examples of documentation can be arts and crafts, certificates, testimonies and endorsements, military records, writing samples, diplomas, works of art, etc.

When preparing to seek experiential learning credits, contact your degree program for details and instructions. Generally, students are encouraged to enroll in a portfolio assessment course where they will learn how to construct a portfolio for a review committee.

If the review committee determines the student's portfolio qualifies for college credit, the student will be awarded credits to apply toward a degree. Portfolios consist of four elements:

(1) request for credits, (2) a resume, (3) a narrative essay on the subject you are seeking credit for , and (4) documentation.

For additional information regarding portfolio preparation, see the following.

Earn Credit for What You Know, by Lois Lamdin, available from:

Council for Adult & Experiential Learning
55 East Monroe Street/Suite 1930
Chicago, Ill 60603

"Portfolio Video Seminar & Printed Study Guide," available from:

> Follet's Bookstore
> Governors State University (IL)
> 1-800/GSU-8GSU Ext.4588

Experiential Learning Guidebook, by William Kemble, available from:

> National College Studies
> Student Assistance Division/Dept. 8G1
> Saugerties, NY 12477

Chapter Twelve

Prison College Programs

The most desirable option for acquiring college credits in prison is prison college programs. Through these programs incarcerated students receive classroom instruction from local college and university professors. Classes are usually held once per week in the evening, and, depending on the program, students from the sponsoring college or university may join the incarcerated students in the classes at the prison. Prison college programs are funded by private grants that pay for incarcerated students' books and tuition.

Some prison college programs in the United States offer degrees. In this chapter we will look at two successful programs—one that awards degrees and one that doesn't—that you can refer back to later if you decide to develop a prison college program at your facility(see chapter 14 Developing Prison College Programs).

According to Jeff Gerritt, a Detroit Free Press (MI) editorial writer, Temple University professor Lori Pompa created a national model [for prison college programs] in 2003/04 when she used a Soros Justice Fellowship to start Inside-Out Prison Exchange Program. The program, currently offered in at least 17 states, brings free and incarcerated students together in classes like sociology and political science. The program doesn't award degrees, but students do receive three transferable college credits per course.

As I write this section on the Inside-Out program, a photo from the National Lifers of America, Inc. newsletter lies on my desk. The closing ceremonies are poignantly captured in the small black and white photocopy of 15 incarcerated students accompanied by 15 free students, the course professor, a University of Michigan chancellor, a Department of Corrections liaison, a judge, a state representative and three state senators. This photo reminds me of the many people who want to see incarcerated students succeed.

The Prison University Project (PUP) is another program that you can later refer to if you decide to develop a prison college program at your facility. The PUP newsletter describes the program as follows:

Our Mission

The mission of the Prison University Project is to provide excellent higher education programs to people incarcerated at San Quentin State Prison; to create a replicable model forsuch programs; and to stimulate public awareness and meaningful dialogue about higher education and criminal justice in California.

Our central goals are to educate and challenge students intellectually; to prepare them to become leaders, within and beyond their own communities, both inside and outside of prison; and to provide them with the skills to obtain meaningful employment and economic stability post-release.

Program Description

The College Program at San Quentin is the central project of the Prison University Project. It provides approximately 12 college courses each semester in the humanities, social sciences, math and science, as well as intensive college preparatory courses in math and English, to over 200 students. It is the only on-site, degree-granting higher education program in all of California's 33 state prisons. The Program is an extension site of Patten University in Oakland, CA.

Students

In order to enroll, students must hold either a high school diploma or a GED. No consideration is given to length of sentence or commitment offense. All students begin in the College Preparatory Program, unless they place directly into credit classes through exam. Students range in age from 22 to 72; the average age is 36. Approximately 32% are white, 37% are black, 18% are Hispanic, 7% are Asian and 6% identify themselves as "other." San Quentin's entire prisoner population is classified as male.

Faculty and Staff

All instructors in the Program work as volunteers; most are graduate students or faculty from UC Berkeley, San Francisco State University, University of San Francisco, Stanford University, and St. Mary's College. All primary instructors in credit earning classes hold at least a master's degree in the given field.

Funding

Because no state or federal funding is available for prison higher education in California, the Program is supported entirely through donations from individuals, private foundations, and corporations. Students in the Program pay no fees or tuition. All textbooks and school supplies are provided by the Prison University Project; the bulk of all books are donated by the publishers. (2) (Reprinted with permission.)

Chapter Thirteen

How to Pay for College

After you have committed to acquiring an education, after you have networked with dozens of people to make your college dream a reality, after you have researched every collegiate option and program, the big question still will be: How are you going to pay for college? Since 1994, when Pell Grants for prisoners were discontinued, incarcerated students throughout the country have pondered this question; for without tuition even the most committed incarcerated student will be as barred from official academic participation as any other inmate. Thus, this section will provide three of the best ways known to pay for college in prison.

However, if you are within two years of being released, you should begin preparing for college in society rather than in prison. The process for getting into school as an inmate—who doesn't already have tuition—may take two or more years, so prisoners who are nearing release should concentrate on preparing for the college entrance exam by developing their skills in math, English and writing.

If you are one of the fortunate ones who will be blessed with the opportunity to attend college outside of prison, congratulations. Please take time to consider the following financial aid information taken from the United States Department of Education publication <u>Funding Education Beyond High School: The Guide to Federal Students Aid.</u>

What is Federal Student Aid?

Federal student aid is financial assistance through the U.S. Department of Education available to eligible students enrolled in an eligible programs as regular students at schools participating in our federal student aid programs.

Federal student aid covers school expenses such as tuition and fees, room and board, books and supplies and transportation. This aid can also help you pay for a computer and dependent child-care expenses. (Note that accepting any Title IV student financial aid does not commit the student to military or other government service.) (1)

What is a Federal Pell Grant?

- Pell Grants are the foundation of federal student financial aid, to which aid from other federal and non-federal sources might be added.

- Pell Grants are generally awarded only to undergraduate students—those who haven't earned a bachelor's or graduate degree.

- In some limited cases, however, you might receive a Pell Grant if you're enrolled in a post baccalaureate teacher certificate program.

- Amounts can change yearly, The maximum award for the 2007-08 award year was $4,310. [Awards for 2010/11 are up to $5,500.] 2

Basic eligibility requirements:

- Demonstrate financial need.
- Be a U.S. citizen or eligible noncitizen (for most programs) with a valid Social Security number (SSN)
- Be working toward a degree or certificate in an eligible program

- Show, by one of the following means, that you're qualified to obtain a postsecondary education:

- Have a high school diploma or a General Education Development (GED) certificate

- Meet other standards that your state establishes and that we have approved.

- Maintain satisfactory academic progress once in school. (3)

How much financial aid can I get?

Pell Grant

- Pell Grant award amounts can change yearly, but Pell Grant awards for the 2007-08 award year (July 1, 2007 to June 30, 2008) ranged from $400 to $4,310. [Awards for 2010/11 are up to $5,500].

- How much grant aid you get depends on:

  - Your EFC [Expected Family Contribution].

  - Your cost of attendance.

  - Whether you are a full-time or part-time student.

  - Whether you attend school for a full academic year or less.

- You may receive only one Pell Grant in an award year.

- You may not receive Pell Grant funds from more than one school at a time. (4)

How Do I Apply For Federal Student Aid?

1. Get free information and help from your school counselor, the financial aid office at the college or career school you plan to attend, or the U.S. Department of Education, Federal Student Aid at www.FederalStudentAid.ed.gov or 1-800-4 FED-AID (1-800-433-3243). Free help is available any time during the application process. You should never have to pay for help.

2. Get a Federal Student Aid PIN, a personal identification number. A PIN lets you apply, "sign" your online Free Application for Federal Student Aid (FAFSA), make corrections to your application information, and more – all online. Apply for a PIN at www.pin. ed.gov.

3. Collect the documents needed to apply, including income tax returns and W-2 forms (and other records of income). A full list of what you need is at www.fafsa.ed.gov. Tax return not completed at the time you apply? Estimate the tax information, apply, and correct information later.

4. Complete the FAFSA between Jan.1, 2008 and June 30. 2009 (no exceptions to either date!) [They mean that you have to submit your paperwork during the first half of the

year]. BUT, apply as soon as possible on or after Jan. 1 to meet school and state aid deadlines-----Apply online (the faster and easier way) by going to www.fafsa.ed.gov.

5. Federal Student Aid will send you a Student Aid Report (SAR) ---which is a summary of the information from your FAFSA. Review you SAR, and if necessary, make changes or corrections and submit your SAR for reprocessing. Your complete, correct SAR will contain your Expected Family Contribution (EFC)—the number used to determine your federal student aid eligibility.

6. If you are selected for verification, your school's financial aid office will ask you to submit tax returns and other documents, as appropriate. Be sure to meet the school's deadlines, or you will not receive federal student aid.

7. Whether you're selected for verification or not, make sure the financial aid office at the school has all the information needed to determine your eligibility.

8. **All students:** Contact the financial aid office if you have any questions about the aid being offered.

    First-time students: Review award letters from schools and compare the aid being offered. Decide which school to attend based on a combination of (a) how well the school suits your needs (programs of study and academics) and (b) its affordability after all aid is taken into account.

You also might be able to get financial aid from your state government, your school or a private scholarship. Research nonfederal aid early---- Be sure to meet all application deadlines! (5)

Because money matters are involved in this section, readers are cautioned and encouraged to consult their state and institutional policy directive and appropriate staff and prison personnel to determine whether the methods featured herein are acceptable to their correctional system. Some incarcerated students find that subtle changes to the methods bring them into compliance with policy regulations; therefore, careful study and cultivation of these techniques can produce promising results in almost any American penal institution.

Chapter Fourteen

How to Find Sponsors

In 2005 I enrolled in a correspondence career institute; about six months later I earned a paralegal certificate (see example 1). That experience of studying for long hours---followed by earning good grades---increased my self-esteem; and by the end of the course, all I wanted to do was go to college. There was just one problem: I didn't have any money.

After careful consideration, I decided to simply ask people for help. I wrote a ten page letter (see example 2), that explained who I was, what I was trying to do, and why I was trying to do it. Later—after I realized no one was going to read that many pages—I condensed the letter to a single page (see example 3). In addition to that letter, I also drafted letters to university faculty requesting assistance (see example 4). But it was the letter to my family and friends that initially got me in school (see example 5).

In Prisoners' Guerrilla Handbook to Correspondence Programs in the United States and Canada, Jon Marc Taylor, arguably the country's leading expert on incarcerated education, says:

> I financed my graduate degree by writing to churches throughout the state seeking tuition assistance. Explaining who I was, where I was at, and what I was trying to accomplish, many congregations graciously supported my quest. Included in my mailing were copies of my transcripts, resume, and references. Finally, I arranged for my mentor to receive and disburse all educational funds. This moderated suspicions of a scam, and recruited an outside advocate for the cause of my education. There are literally thousands of congregations and hundreds of service groups in each state. Arrange a contact package (remembering you are basically saying: "Hi, I'm a convict who wants to go to college. Please give me money to do so.") that best presents your cause, is designed to alleviate as many fears from the recipients' mind as possible, and is as simple a plan that will work in the circumstances you are constrained within.
>
> In Indiana, I had a success rate of two-percent of contacted churches sponsoring at least one or more classes. In Missouri, on the other hand,

utilizing the refined contact package, I could not enlist a single sponsor out of three-hundred-plus churches contacted. (1)

Like Mr. Taylor, I've had my share of failed attempts to recruit sponsors also; for instance, in 2006 I wrote an advocacy article for Prison Living Magazine (see example 6) about the Greyhound rescue program at my facility. A year later my parents and Uncle Kermett paid for 100 sponsorship packets (see example 7) to be mailed to Greyhound organizations throughout the country. Unfortunately, after all of the time and expense, not a single person sponsored me. Since that experience, I have advocated carefully considering fund raising endeavors rather than merely reaching out to anyone who might listen. However, I know of at least one person who has succeeded in acquiring tuition by mass marketing himself.

In Prison Living Magazine, Troy Evans describes how, through a traditional Scholarship foundation, he acquired funding for college.

July 16, 1997….a guard sticks his head in my cell and tells me that my counselor wants to see me immediately. He says he received a phone call from a scholarship committee chairman with a national association in Auburn, Al… My counselor says that association is interested in helping me with my schooling. And then it all comes back to me; six months ago, I spent every free minute I had---14, 16 or 18 hours a day….filling out applications, writing essays, begging, pleading and selling myself to absolutely every private scholarship available. But I was a con, a felon; no one wanted to take a chance on me. Each day at mail call, I received a stack of rejection letters. "Thanks, but no thanks". One week after being called to my counselor's office, I received a letter and a check from that association for one class. The letter states that although I did not meet the selection criteria, they were so impressed with what I was attempting to do that they were going to award me a special stipend. I take that one class and send them my report card. They then send me a check for two classes and once again I send them my report card. It snowballs to the point that they are funding entire semesters and the end result of their help is me walking out those gates of prison with two college degrees, both earned with a 4.0 GPA and placement on the Dean's and President's lists. (2)

Like Mr. Evans, I too struggled to find sponsors. After I finished my first two college courses—also with a 4.0 GPA—I ordered my college transcripts (see example 8) and composed a letter of appreciation to my sponsors (see example 9). I didn't have enough support to immediately get back into school after the first two courses, but I stayed focused and got to work on other constructive projects.

I wrote a small book titled <u>Catholicism in Prison</u> that is currently being reviewed for endorsement by a Roman Catholic bishop and I designed parochial school activity sheets (see example 10) for Catholic school teachers. I offered the sheets to teachers for a donation of any amount, but again, I didn't get any responses, Mr. Taylor says:

> While funding….will most likely be you're most difficult task in continuing your education, it is not impossible. Be creative. be persistent. And be honest in where you are, what you want to accomplish, and how you progress. You will be surprised in the amount of support you can receive when you believe in yourself and strive valiantly towards your dreams. Share your grades and papers with your friends, family, and sponsors. Seek to include them with your life and success. I have been blessed to make many lifelong friends in my search for funding. I pray you are as lucky. (3)

During the past three years I have learned that fund raising for college isn't merely a matter of whether you get the money; it's a matter of whether you maintained integrity during the process. For instance, did you study for college even when you didn't have the money to take the next course? Did you engage in productive activities when all of your efforts to get in school were failing? Did you charitably share your new-found knowledge with others? The answers to these questions reveal character and priorities; consequently, I encourage you to make the most of every day because, even if you don't see immediate rewards, your efforts will add up and you will attract new sponsors—or at least increase the measure of trust your current sponsors have in you.

Blackstone Career Institute

Established 1890

Confers this Diploma of
Legal Assistant/Paralegal
upon

Bruce C. Michaels

who has fulfilled all the requirements prescribed by the School and is entitled
to all of the honors rights and privileges thereunto appertaining.

In Testimony Whereof *this recognition of achievement is*

Given this 4th day of October 2005

President

Valerie L. Behrle B.S., M.Ed.
Director of Education

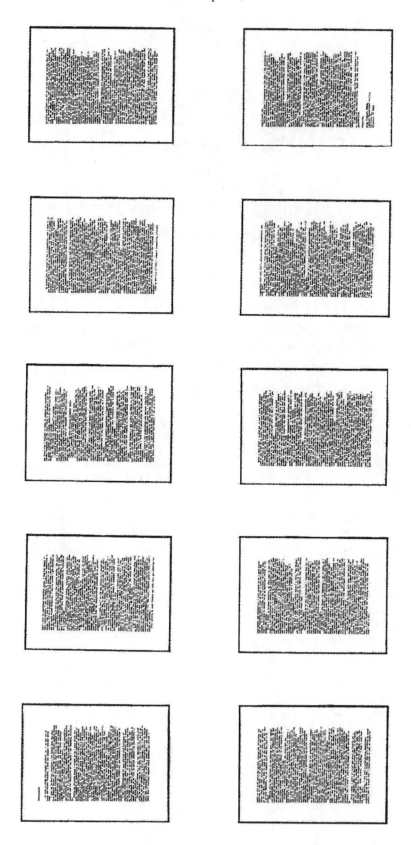

College in Prison

(Example 3)

Dear Friend,

My name is Bruce Micheals. I am a convicted murderer and have been incarcerated in the Michigan Department of Corrections since 1989. I am writing this letter as a brief introduction in hopes of providing you with an accurate description of me.

I grew up in a respectable, loving, blue collar family and community. I was raised to believe in God, to be honest and to make responsible decisions. As a child I was self absorbed (though polite) and very selfish. As a teenager I constantly lived in fear of what others thought of me, and I believed money could solve all of my problems. From my inexperienced perspective acquiring money seemed to be the only way to be successful in life and to make people like me. I worked several jobs, went to school and committed crimes regularly.

At 16 years old I was convicted of robbery, murder, and other related offenses. Felony convictions and incarceration, however, did not change my mind concerning money and its miracle cure possibilities. In prison I became even more corrupt and further embraced the criminal mentality. I spent 10 years in maximum security, several in administrative segregation (the hole), and was nearly killed on a number of occasions.

Over the years I have learned from skilled career criminals and witnessed the results of the "Game" in my life and others'. My parents raised me well but I rejected their advice. Today I shamefully look back with remorse and regret upon many hard lessons. I am no longer a criminal: I do not believe in, participate in, or condone criminal activity or philosophy. I am in prison trying to pay my debt to society and to the victims of my crimes---even though I will never be able to give them back the life they deserve. I am sorry for what I have done and I make no excuses for it.

Growing up in prison is not an easy thing to do, nor is rehabilitating a criminal mind, but I have done (and continue to do) both. If possible, I would like to spend the rest of my life helping others who also struggle with a criminal mentality. I am a firm believer that people ultimately do whatever they want to, and if they can be persuaded to stop wanting to be criminal, I believe they will eventually become responsible.

Today I am happily married, pursuing an education, and devoted to being a productive and responsible person. My wife has approximately 11 years of college experience and has been very supportive of my efforts. My family is supportive as well, but the support of my peers is a welcome surprise. I get plenty of resistance from young aspiring career criminals, but most of the mature criminals that I talk to understand what I am doing, and though they aren't prepared to commit to it themselves, I nevertheless appreciate their moral support.

I first attempted to rehabilitate in 1996, but it took until 2002 before I was able to firmly say to myself that I would not freely commit another crime for the rest of my life. My hope is that I will be able to influence others to join me in the commitment. For me, and so many others, the past is a dirty word. Through diligent efforts and support, however, I believe even people as messed up as me can make the future better.

Bruce Micheals

(Example 4)

Ms. Vanisse Beols
Assist. Dir., Enrollment Services
000 Street
P.O. Box 000
City, St, Zip

Bruce C. Micheals, Jr. #208666
Lakeland Correctional Facility
141 First St.
Coldwater, MI 49036

Dear Ms. Beols,

I am writing to ask if you will sponsor me to go to college. Please forgive my lack of niceties, but it is true. I don't want to die one day as an uneducated prisoner with nothing to show for his time. I was sentenced to spend the rest of my life in prison when I was 16 years old, and after 17 years of incarceration, I just want to do something positive with myself.

I won't pull your leg: I have been a very bad person. But I have also spent many years (more than a decade) examining my conscience and making honest changes to be the very best person I can be. I have many honest years under my belt, and I have a deep need in my heart to do something with the ones I have left.

I'm passionate about juvenile intervention and rehabilitation. I believe I could have been saved. Thus, I am writing an anthology of 20 true short stories about my peers in here and their experiences with irrevocable decisions. 15 of the 20 stories are finished; when the anthology is completed, I intend to send copies to the maximum security boy's training school W.J. Maxey---staff there have already reviewed some of the material and expressed interest in it. This project isn't much, but it is something.

In addition to the anthology, I am also working on other writing projects that promote criminal contemplation and rehabilitation. By using my experience and knowledge of the criminal mentality, I try to capture the essential things relevant to lasting change and put them in stories that readers with similar struggles might benefit from. I believe a formal education will make me a better writer, and as a writer I hope to bring some sort of good out of this terrible situation.

My father is holding all of the money for my college fund. When I get enough for the first two courses he will forward the funds and I will get the courses 4-6 weeks later. After that I will start raising funds for the next installment of courses.

As soon as I finish a set of courses (and get the grades back), I will forward the grades, receipts for the courses, and any other relevant information to my sponsors along with a description of the next set of courses I am raising funds for.

A long time ago I heard someone say: "I don't mind helping someone, as long as he is willing to help himself." If that is how you feel, too, please consider helping me. I am doing the best I can to gain the skills I need, and if you help me, I will reward your kindness with good grades and a lifetime of thoughtful contributions of my own—like the anthology.

Sincerely,

Bruce Micheals

College in Prison

The Bruce Micheals College Fund

Yes, I would like to support Bruce Micheals college endeavor. Enclosed is my contribution of $----. -- I can be contacted at the following address for up-dates on Bruce's progress.

Name

Address

City/St/Zip

Send cash, check or money order made payable to:
Bruce Micheals, Sr., Street, City, St, Zip

Bruce C. Micheals

(Example 5)

Dear_____,

How are you? I am well. Amy and the boys are doing good. I'm prepared to start college through Ohio University and I would like to know if you will sponsor me for $20 a year. If that is too much, maybe $10 would be better?

Over the years I have had time to reflect on the decisions I made as a juvenile and I have worked diligently to become a better person. Last year Amy paid $800 for me to get paralegal training; I finished the one year course in six months with a 95% GPA. From that training I went on to write almost 50 small legal reports on various aspects of the law pertaining to prisoners, and 27 of the reports may be available for purchase by prisoners in the near future. I bring this up as an example of my intentions. If I am given the opportunity to gain an education I will use it in a positive and productive way.

After taking the paralegal course I began studying English out of a dozen or more books, and I discovered that I love the subject. I have since joined a writers' workshop and decided to develop my skills further. Currently I have three poems in an anthology and am writing a small book for Incarcerated Juveniles about irrevocable decisions that feature real life stories about the prisoners who live around me. The publication will have photos on every page and offer relevant questions for counselors or teachers to discuss with the kids. So far I have received enthusiastic support by three people who work in juvenile facilities, as well as encouragement from others who work with troubled teens in other capacities as well.

I am sentenced to die in prison, I accept my punishment, but while I am here I want to use my time wisely. I know what the criminal life has to offer, I look into the hollow eyes of my peers everyday, but I want more for myself and them.

Prison doesn't have to be a place of misery and sorrow; it can be a place of healing and charitable productivity.

I am going to make something of myself and I would like you to help me.

I need 250 people to pledge $20 per year for five years. I am enclosing a pledge form for you to fill out and return to Amy with your contribution (if you choose to support my endeavor), and next year before I ask for another $20 I will show you what I have done with the $20 you gave me this year. My goal is to get the highest GPA possible. I want you to know how much I appreciate your support and by applying myself I hope to earn high marks that will later translate into positive ventures.

If you have any suggestions on how I might further raise funds please share them with me. As a prisoner I am not eligible for a PELL Grant or student loan so my options are to either raise the money myself or not go to school. Some people might prefer that I forego an education altogether and simply do my time, but I have done far too much wrong already in my life to squander what is left of it like that. To me life is very simple: I have done wrong, I don't like it, so now I have to do what is right. I believe anyone can be productive and responsible, even me; and I hope you will believe and help me too. I will do my best not to let you down.

Sincerely,

Chris

P.S. As you can see this is primarily a form letter, with so many loved ones to write I am trying to save time and money, I hope you don't mind. My immediate goal is to acquire the support of friends and family; the majority of my sponsors later will probably be people who have never heard of me before, so I need a strong core group of sponsors to show faith in me and what I am endeavoring to accomplish. You are my family, and though I have done more harm to it than good, I need you to help me make things better. I'm 32 years old, I'm not the 16 year old of yesterday, and I have something meaningful to contribute to the world—I just need your help to get started.

---cut here---

The 2006 Bruce Micheals College Fund-Raiser Pledge Form

Yes, I support Bruce Michaels's college endeavor and would like to contribute:

____$20

____$10

_____ Other (Please specify amount at bottom of this form.)

Name

Address

City/St/Zip

Send cash, check or money order made payable to:
Amy Micheal's, Street Address, City, ST, Zip Code.

College in Prison

(Example 7)

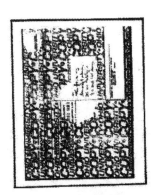

Ohio University Print Date: 11/05/2007 Page: 1 of 1

DEBRA M. BENTON
UNIVERSITY REGISTRAR

ACADEMIC RECORD OF: MICHEALS, BRUCE C

IDENTIFICATION NUMBER: ▬▬▬▬

UNDERGRADUATE RECORD ONLY

PFX NUM COURSE TITLE	HRS GR PTS CD	PFX NUM COURSE TITLE	HRS GR PTS CD

CURRENT PROGRAM(S) OF STUDY
SPECIAL STUDENT MAJOR (ND1202)

*********** U N D E R G R A D U A T E ***********

FALL QUARTER 2007-08 (09/04/2007 - 11/21/2007)
QUARTER IN PROGRESS
ENG 150 DEVELOPMENTAL WRITING 4.0 A 16.00 C
MATH 101 BASIC MATHEMATICS 4.0 A 16.00 C

TERM: HRS A 8.0|HRS E 8.0|GP 32.000|GPA 4.000

******** E N D O F T R A N S C R I P T ********

Thus far, as my transcript shows, I am holding a 4.0 Grade Point Average.

ISSUED TO: BRUCE MICHAELS # 208666
141 FIRST ST
COLDWATER MI 49036

College in Prison

(Example 9)

Dear _____,

11/21/07

How are you? I am well--working hard. Recently, I finished my first two college courses--the ones you sponsored. A copy of my transcript from Ohio University is enclosed; I finished both classes with A's (4.0 GPA).

Developing solid study habits and contending with the prison atmosphere was a challenge, but I am pleased with the results, and I would like to continue if you and my other sponsors are still willing to support my endeavor.

Over the past year I haven't merely acquired knowledge; rather, I have attempted to use what I have learned to help others. For instance, last year the MODC began a program to contribute to the national Greyhound rescue effort. I contributed to the cause by writing a promotional article (enclosed) for a national prison magazine.

Additionally, over the past year I have researched more than 100 college level distance learning programs to determine the most cost efficient academic opportunities available to incarcerated students. In doing so, I have discovered numerous options that have encouraged more than a dozen prisoners to join me in pursuing higher education.

However, the past year hasn't been entirely good. Amy and I divorced May, 2007--shortly before my mid-term exams. The break-up was every bit as challenging as the courses; but, considering the outcome, I think Amy and I both earned A's by separating with respect, dignity, love, and affection.

Over the winter I intend to complete a small book for incarcerated Catholics that may be published in 2008. Besides that, I plan to raise money for school and get ready for next year's spring semester.

Last year, when I realized I needed a better education--to pursue a career in writing--I didn't really know whether I'd be able to make it in the competitive academic environment. The experience of this past year, however, has increased my confidence. Thus, starting next spring, I would like to attempt a full course load, which is about three courses per semester.

To maintain that many courses, I will need to attract additional sponsors and maintain the support of the ones I have; consequently, I am in the process of contacting over 300 potential sponsors, acquiring small scholarships and grants, and earning college tuition through professional writing (I got my first check on 11/15/07). So, please, continue to support my education and keep me in your prayers.

Thank you for playing such a crucial role in my efforts.

In gratitude,

Bruce (Chris) Micheals

........Cut here........

The Bruce C. Micheals, Jr. College Fund

Yes, I would like to support Bruce's college endeavor. Enclosed is my contribution of $_____. Send my up-dates (regarding Bruce's progress) to the following address:

Name
Address
City/ST/Zip

Send cash, check, or money order made payable to:

Drive-Through and I at the fish pond

Bruce C. Micheals

(Example 10)

Bruce C. Michaels, Jr. #208666
Lakeland Correctional Facility
141 First St.
Coldwater, MI 49036
1/11/08

Dear Principal------------------------,

I'm an inmate in the Michigan Department of Corrections. We aren't acquainted, but I'm writing to ask if you will help me with a project I am working on. The project relates to my rehabilitation –particularly my education.

In 1989 I was sentenced to spend the rest of my life in prison for crimes I did, in fact, commit; I was 16 years old at the time, and I was extremely corrupt and impulsive. However, much has changed over the past 18 years, namely, I have matured, become Catholic, and acquired a healthy regard for academics. Consequently, I recently enrolled in Ohio University's College Program for the Incarcerated (CPI), and I earned A's in both of the courses I took. I'm majoring in journalism and behavioral science because I want to write about criminal rehabilitation, especially as it relates to juveniles and our faith; but college is terribly expensive and I'm trying to earn tuition—which brings me to the point of this letter.

I am trying to raise funds for school by offering principals, such as yourself, a series of reproducible activity sheets on the Doctors of the Church (samples enclosed) for elementary and junior-high school students. My options for earning money are limited, so I'm doing everything I can to acquire tuition—writing books, articles, pamphlets, even activity sheets— but I have only had a few articles published, so far; thus, please consider returning the attached subscription form with a donation of <u>any amount,</u> and I will send you new activity sheets—as I finish them—after each semester of school.

May Our Lady keep you in her Immaculate Heart,

Bruce C. Micheals, Jr.

Doctors of the Church Activity Sheets

Yes, I would like to subscribe to the Doctors of the Church Activity Sheets series. Enclosed is my donation of $----------. Please send my activity sheets to the address below.

Name_____

Address_____

City/St/Zip_____

Send cash, check or money order made payable to:
Bruce C. Micheals, Sr, Address, City, St, Zip

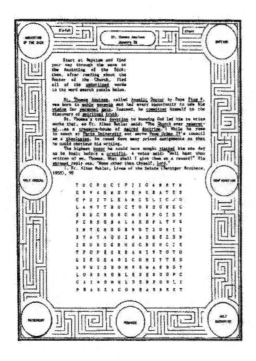

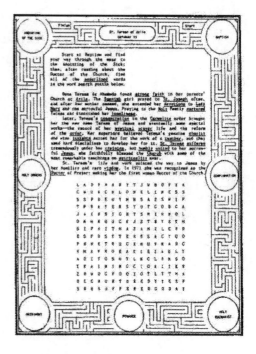

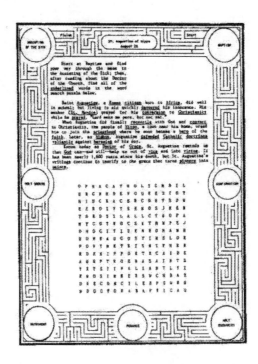

Chapter Fifteen

Developing a Prison College Program

Getting a college program at your facility is tantamount to acquiring full scholarships for yourself and your peers. College programs often pay for tuition, books, and supplies, leaving students free to study and learn.

To develop such a program at your facility, begin by talking to your principal: propose researching successful prison college programs and the potential for establishing a college program at your facility. Avoid soliciting the principal's support too early; rather, seek only the principal's opinion and advice—something your principal will be more inclined to give.

Once you have spoken with your principal, contact some prison college programs, and ask them for information regarding how they got established. By doing this, you will learn how to design your program. After you have contacted the programs, write to your local community college professors, and tell them about your research; ask them to help you develop a program at your facility, and ask for suggestions on how you should proceed.

Next, ask your principal to be the staff sponsor of your college program. Then, explain what you have learned about the programs you wish to pattern yours after. Include a list of the professors who are interested in helping to develop the program, and provide a brief report on how you believe a program could be established at your facility.

While you are tending to the preliminaries mentioned in the preceding paragraphs, you should also begin studying grant proposal writing books. If your library does not have books on this subject, ask your librarian to borrow books on grant writing through inter-library loan, or contact your local book seller for a list of current available titles.

After you learn how to write a grant proposal, draft one, and send it to your principal and the professors. Ask them to review it and to offer suggestions on how the proposal might be improved. When you receive their responses, consider every suggestion carefully, and make note of the parties who seem the most supportive of your endeavor.

After you have thoroughly revised and refined the proposal, ask your most supportive professor to submit the proposal to grant foundations. The professor's credentials—a master's or doctoral degree—will significantly increase the odds of your grant proposal getting approved.

Chapter Sixteen

Earning College Scholarships In Prison

Everyone knows that it is difficult to acquire financial aid for college in prison; however, if you are reasonably rehabilitated and prepared to do collegiate level work, you may be eligible for a scholarship. I have included a mock-scholarship application at the end of this chapter (see example 1) for you to reference later. This is only an example of the information scholarship committees ask for, but if you structure your life in accordance with it, you will not only become a great scholarship candidate, you will also become a great person.

Be aware, however, the criteria for individual scholarships usually favors high school students and will often weed out felons; thus I suggest applying for "special needs" funding (i.e. financial aid that is based on your personal need rather than a specific scholarship's interest). By submitting such a request to a scholarship committee, you will avoid the strict scholarship criteria that often disqualifies incarcerated students and you will get a unique opportunity to introduce yourself to people who are capable of paying for some or all of your educational expenses.

Your financial aid request should at least include the following.

1. A current photo that favorably depicts you;

2. A facts sheet that includes your full name, inmate number, address, date of birth, social security number, gender, educational history, major (or intended major), list of academic awards, religious activities, charitable contributions and work history;

3. An account statement that shows your financial need;

4. Reference letters from two or three professionals who the committee can contact to verify your character; do not use friends or family members. Your school principal, the librarian, a professor, or other professional (see chapters 5 and 6) who is aware of your academic interests will make a

good reference. If you have sponsors, consider asking one of them to write a letter of endorsement for you;

5. an essay or letter that pleads your case for financial aid (if your essay or letter exceeds two hand written pages, or one and a half typed pages, revise it. Busy people want the facts in fast pitch; if you give it to them; they will reward you with their attention).

Scholarships are not easy to get, but persistent prisoners do get them (see example 2). The best times to apply are before February and September of each year.
Responses can take up to six months, so I suggest submitting requests until you get accepted.

To get started, check out books on grants, scholarships, and student financial aid from your library or interlibrary loan service. I recommend using the <u>Ferguson Career Resource Guide to Grants, Scholarships, and other Financial Resources,</u> but most current scholarship directories will provide hundreds of promising tuition sources. In 2010 five of my peers in the college group and I were awarded over $8,000 in scholarships, this isn't counting the support we received from our sponsors. Use this book to join the academic renaissance.

"Do what you can,
with what you have,
right where you are."

Theodore Roosevelt

Bruce C. Micheals

(Example 1)

The (Name) Scholarship Fund
Address
1-800-000-0000
www.(name).org

The purpose of the (name) Scholarship Fund
is to make higher education available, through financial aid,
to high school students.

REQUIREMENTS
High School Senior
Community involvements or religious activity
Financial need
High school transcripts
Three letters of recommendation

Deadline
Applications must be received by the scholarship committee by Feb 12th.

Rules
(Name) foundation will make awards by April 1st. Submission of an
Application constitutes permission for (name) foundation to use scholarship
candidate's name and/or likeness for promotion, advertising, and trade.
Awards are not transferable. Scholarship open to residents of the
continental United States only. Awards good only for use at accredited
colleges and universities.

Award
Ten $1,000 awards per year.
Proof of college registration necessary prior to receipt of award.

College in Prison

(Example 1)

On a separate sheet of paper provide the following information.

Personal Information
Name, address, phone, date of birth, social security number, gender.

Education
Name of high school attended, address, principal, student advisor.
When do your expect to begin collegiate studies?
List your extracurricular activities.
List awards you have received.

Religious and Community
List your religious activities.
List your community activities (civic or political)

Work History
List the jobs you have held.

Financial Information
Parent's names, address(s), phone(s), occupation(s), and their annual income(s).

Additional Information
How did you learn about the (name) scholarship fund?
In 500 words or less, print clearly an essay entitled "How I Intend To Use My College Education To Help My Community."
Print the names of the three people who wrote letters of recommendation for you and enclose the letters with this application.

Privacy Act Statement
Under the authority of Article 5 U.S.C. 301, Information Act, your name, address, and your telephone number may be requested. This information is used for the purpose of keeping the records of all applicants, forwarding names to other available funds and for (name's) promotional purposes. Any individual who does not sign this privacy statement will be excluded from the list that will be sent to other scholarship funds and other (name) activities.

I understand the information in this application packet, and the information that I have provided is correct to the best of my knowledge.

Signature/Date

Please attach a photo of yourself and mail to the address above.

Bruce C. Micheals

(Example 2)

life after prison

Troy Evans
Author

Troy Evans was a self-employed addict, drug dealer, gambler and thief for more than 15 years. Ultimately, his disregard of values and discipline resulted in a 13-year federal prison sentence. Following a six-month crime spree, which included five armed bank robberies in three states, Evans' self-destructive lifestyle was brought to an end. He soon found himself within the razor wire of the Federal Correctional Complex in Florence, Colo.

Evans was determined that his time behind bars would not be wasted. He chose Education as his saving grace, despite the elimination of Federal Pell Grants for the incarcerated. Undeterred, Evans set out to secure funding on his own through scholarships, grants and foundation assistance. After six months of submitting applications, writing essays, begging, pleading and selling, Evans landed his first scholarship for one class. That was a beginning and when Evans walked out the doors of prison, he carried with him two degrees, both obtained with a 4.0 GPA and placement on the Dean's and President's lists.

Since his release in 1999, Evans relates his story and message for life change on the national speakers' circuit and has taken the corporate, association and education speaking platforms by storm. He has spoken to bankers, credit union personnel, school administrators, teachers, counselors/social workers, HR professionals, teens and law enforcement professionals. Evans shows how the keys to his success in prison are the keys to his success today, and how these lessons can be applied to escaping the "prisons within ourselves." Evans' first book "From Desperation to Dedication: Lessons You Can Bank On" has become a best seller. In addition, he has been a guest on "Good Morning America", CNN and featured in such publications as *The New Yorker, Washington Post, Chicago Tribune, New York Daily News, Newsday* and numerous other periodicals.

Evans resides in Phoenix, with his wife Pam and his dog Archibald.

The Evans Group
3104 E. Camelback Rd., #436
Phoenix, AZ 85016
602-265-6855
Fax 602-285-1474
troy@troyevans.com
www.troyevans.com

16 prison living

Feature Article

I can link my crimes and incarceration to the decision I made as a teenager to experiment with drugs. Drugs eventually became more important than anything or anyone else and bank robbery became a means to feed my habit for another 30 to 60 days.

On March 20, 1992, I was convicted of five armed bank robberies, over a six-month crime spree. I was 28 years old and sentenced to 13 years and one month at Federal Correctional Institution in Florence, Colo.; which is the same complex that would later hold Timothy McVeigh and Terry Nichols.

> My dad said, "Anything in this life that is worthwhile, really worthwhile, is never easy."

During my five-month trial, I experience an "awakening" and this transformation is fueled by three things. The first is the "dead time" in prison, which literally hangs in the air. I would sit in the common areas and see guys play cards or watch TV for up to 16 hours a day. Some of these guys do this for five, ten or 15 years. I could not fathom spending all of those years in that fashion. The second thing that fueled this awakening is my 7-year-old son, Eric. I find that I have the responsibility to influence my far-away son in a positive way. And the third thing that fueled my awakening is something my Dad used to say when I was a kid; something that I lost track of during my teens and early 20s, but something that I came to believe and rely on during those years of incarceration. He

98

TROY EVANS

said, "Anything in this life that is worthwhile is never easy." I had always taken the easy road. The easy road is the drug use, lying, stealing and cheating. It doesn't take a special individual to travel that path.

My awakening is education. Education is what I am going to use as a tool to make a negative situation positive. But first I have a decision to make: Should I take the plea agreement that the prosecution has offered? My options are pleading to 157 months or waiting for the outcome of a Supreme Court decision that would directly effect my sentence. My attorney tells me to wait for the Supreme Court outcome because her sources say they are leaning towards a favorable outcome. She gives me three days to think about it. Each of those three nights, a strong feeling tells me to take the plea agreement. I have no idea where it is coming from, but I know it is strong and clear. I inform my attorney of my decision and against her recommendation, was sentenced to the 157 months. Four weeks later I discover that the Supreme Court ruling would have resulted in my being sentenced to 53 years. The judge in my case would not have had a choice; he would have to follow mandatory sentencing guidelines.

Fast-forward to July 16, 1997. I have been locked up four and one-half years when a guard sticks his head in my cell and tells me that my counselor wants to see me immediately. He says he received a phone call from a scholarship committee chairman with a national association in Auburn, Ala. My counselor says the association is interested in helping me with my schooling. And then it all comes back to me; six months ago, I spent every free minute I had - 14, 16 or 18 hours a day sitting at my tiny little prison desk in my cell, filling out applications, writing essays, begging, pleading and selling myself to absolutely every private scholarship available. But I was a con, a felon; no one wanted to take a chance on me. Each day at mail call, I received a stack of rejection letters. "Thanks, but no thanks." I was two years into my first degree and it was beginning to look like my dream was just not going to happen. One week after being called to my counselor's office, I receive a letter and a check from that association for one class. The letter states that although I did not meet the selection criteria, they were so impressed with what I was attempting to do that they were going to award me a special stipend. I take that one class and send them my report card. They then send me a check for two classes and once again I send them my report card. It snowballs to the point that they are funding entire semesters and the end result of their help is me walking out those gates of prison with two college degrees, both earned with a 4.0 GPA and placement on the Dean's and President's Lists.

Things are moving along wonderfully. I am making my family proud and my son shows a renewed interest in his own education. It becomes something he and I could share; a relationship between us has never been stronger. I cannot be with my boy, but I am doing something with him. Things are going good when a new warden comes to FCI Florence.

He immediately takes a dislike to me. He does not like the fact that I was given extra computer time, extra library time and that I am allowed to receive videotapes through the mail. He tells me that all of these things were coming to an end immediately. I turn to the association who funds my academic career that happens to be well connected politically. Over the next six weeks, 28 Congressman and Senators write and call this warden demanding to know why I am not being allowed to complete my second degree. The warden does not like this. He is not used to answering to anyone and he really does not like the fact that one of his inmates stirred up this hornet's nest. So he puts me under investigation, calls me a risk to the security of the institution and throws me in "the hole." Just when I think things cannot get worse, I am informed that I am being transferred to FCI Englewood. One of oldest prisons within the Federal Bureau of Prisons, built in 1939, it looks like something out of a medieval movie. Once again I ask myself, 'why is this happening?' I can not imagine spending the next five years in these conditions. Well, things happen for a reason. I am at FCI Englewood for three months when I hear my name over the intercom, "Evans #24291-013 report to the records office immediately." When I arrive at the records office, I am told to shut the door and sit. The lady tells me that she just got off the phone with the regional office, they have reviewed my sentence and there has been a mistake. I should not have been sentenced to 13 years, I should have been sentenced to eight. She tells me I am going home in ten days.

If that warden had not disliked me, if I had not been thrown in "the hole" and if I had not been transferred to FCI Englewood, I would have spent an additional five years in federal prison.

Looking back, one thing is perfectly clear: If you are doing the right things, treating others as you would want them to treat you, are fair and are committed to working hard, I can assure you magical things will happen in your life.

> **"If you are doing the right things, magical things will happen in your life.**

FROM DESPERATION TO DEDICATION: LESSONS YOU CAN BANK ON

Troy Evans

Notes

Chapter 8

1. Jon Marc Taylor, <u>Prisoners' Guerrilla Handbook to Correspondence Programs in The United States and Canada</u> (Brunswick, ME: Biddle Publishing Company, 2002), 20.

Chapter 12

1. Jeff Gerritt, "College Goes To Prison," <u>Detroit Free Press,</u> 17, October 2007, editorial

2. "Who We Are And What We Do," <u>Prison University Project,</u> 3, No. 3 (2008): 4.

Chapter 13

1 .U.S. Department of Education, Federal Student Aid, Students Channel, <u>Funding Education Beyond High School: The Guide To Federal Student Aid</u> 2008-09, Washington, D.C., D.C., 2007, xii

2. Federal Student Aid, 6.

3. Federal Student Aid, xiii.

4. Federal Student Aid, 7.

5. Federal Student Aid, xii.

Chapter 14

1. Taylor, 29.

2. Troy Evans, "Life After Prison," <u>Prison Living Magazine</u> 1, no. 3 (2006): 16-17.

3. Taylor, 29.

Disclaimer

This book is designed to provide information about the subject matter covered. It is sold with the understanding that the publisher and author are not engaged in rendering legal, accounting or other professional services. If legal or other expert assistance is required, the services of a competent professional should be sought.

It is not the purpose of this manual to reprint all the information that is otherwise available to incarcerated students but to complement, amplify and supplement other texts. For more information, contact a librarian, academic counselor, or principal.

Earning legitimate college degrees in prison is not a simple, easy endeavor. Anyone who decides to pursue an academic career while incarcerated must expect to invest a lot of time and effort without any guarantee of success. Degrees from regionally accredited colleges and universities are not handed out indiscriminately. To earn degrees incarcerated students must work just as hard, if not harder, than their peers on college campuses.

Every effort has been made to make this book as complete and as accurate as possible. However, there may be mistakes both typographical and in content. Therefore, this text should be used only as a general guide and not as the ultimate source of information and resources on college in prison only up to the printing date.

The purpose of this publication is to educate and entertain. The author and publisher shall have neither liability nor responsibility to any person or entity with respect to any loss or damage caused or alleged to be caused directly or indirectly by the information contained in this book.